T. Fielding.

Pointing Out the Dharmakaya

POINTING OUT THE DHARMAKAYA

Teachings on the Ninth Karmapa's Text

by
Khenchen Thrangu Rinpoche

Oral Translation by Lama Yeshe Gyamtso
Edited and Annotated by Lama Tashi Namgyal

Snow Lion Publications
Ithaca, New York ✦ Boulder, Colorado

Snow Lion Publications
P. O. Box 6483
Ithaca, New York 14851 USA
(607) 273-8519
www.snowlionpub.com

Text designed and typeset by Gopa & Ted2, Inc.

Printed in Canada on acid-free recycled paper.

ISBN 1-55939-203-7

Library of Congress Cataloging-in-Publication Data

Thrangu, Rinpoche, 1933-
  Pointing out the dharmakaya : teachings on the Ninth Karmapa's text / by
Khenchen Thrangu Rinpoche ; oral translation by Lama Yeshe Gyamtso ;
edited and annotated by Lama Tashi Namgyal.
    p. cm.
  Translation of an oral commentary on the Ninth Karmpa's "Phyag rgya
chen po lhan cig skyes sbyor gyi khrid zin bris snying po gsal ba'i sgron me
bdud rtsi'i nying khu chos sku mdzus tshugs su ngo sprod pa."
  ISBN 1-55939-203-7 (alk. paper)
  1. Mahāmudrā (Tantric rite) 2. Dban-phyug-rdo-rje, Karma-pa IX, 1556-
1603. I. Yeshe Gyamtso, Lama, 1959- II. Tashi Namgyal, Lama, 1942-
III. Title.
BQ7699.M34 T475 2003
294.3'4435—dc22

2003017052

CONTENTS

FOREWORD

by His Holiness the Dalai Lama

TIBETAN BUDDHISM encompasses the full range of the Buddha's teachings. It consists of four major traditions, of which the Kagyu tradition traces its origins particularly to the teachings of the great Indian Buddhist masters Tilopa and Naropa. The transmission of these teachings in Tibet goes back to the great translator Marpa, his renowned disciple, the great yogi Milarepa, and his disciple, the teacher Gampopa. The tradition is characterized particularly by the teaching and practice of the Great Seal (mahamudra) and the Six Yogas of Naropa.

This book contains the core of teachings characteristic of the tradition. The text taught here is the Ninth Karmapa Wangchuk Dorje's *Pointing Out the Dharmakaya*. Karmapa Wangchuk Dorje is remembered particularly for his three texts on the Great Seal, or mahamudra, of which this is the most concise. In addition to his renowned writings, he travelled widely and taught, restoring and establishing temples and monasteries wherever he went, particularly in southern Tibet. Indeed, it was he who initiated the foundation of Rumtek Monastery in Sikkim, which has become the seat of the Karmapas in exile.

Mahamudra, an advanced practice whose focus is the nature of the mind, is the principal topic here. Yet it would be wrong to think that it is enough simply to meditate in mahamudra without the necessary foundational practices. As the text shows, its successful practice cannot be separated from cultivating the basic qualities of love, compassion, and the awakening mind of bodhichitta. These are what endow our practice with determination and mental strength. If we cultivate such qualities, then with repeated practice and the passage of time, our tough and unruly minds can be transformed into marvelous states.

The Ninth Karmapa's fundamental text is taught here by the contemporary Kagyu meditation master and scholar, Khenchen Thrangu Rinpoche, who is one of the most learned and experienced of the senior Karma Kagyu teachers living today. Indeed, he is the tutor of the present Seventeenth Karmapa, Ogyen Trinley Dorje.

Readers who are interested in discovering the nature of the mind will find much here in this clear and thorough guide to delight and inspire them.

Tenzin Gyatso
June 7, 2002

PREFACE

WHAT IS CONTAINED HERE is a remarkably extensive and detailed approach to looking at the mind, which represents the teachings on insight [vipashyana] meditation as presented in the tradition of mahamudra. Students who have received over the course of years rather short and pithy introductions to the nature of mind, and introductions to how to look at the mind, will find in this extraordinary set of instructions systematic and comprehensive approaches to ascertaining the mind's true nature, to checking one's experience, and to refining and extending one's insight.

In order to make use of these instructions—in order for these instructions to become something other than a passing academic curiosity—one must first develop the experience of shamatha, or tranquility meditation.

If one can rest undistractedly in an awareness of the present moment, then the vipashyana instructions contained here, when accompanied by the appropriate direct transmission, will not only be of great interest and great benefit but can become the one sufficient path that will lead the practitioner to the understanding, direct experience, and full realization of selflessness, the emptiness of phenomena, and the emptiness of consciousness. If one is still having difficulty resting undistractedly in an awareness of the present moment, one needs to practice shamatha until one can. If one has difficulty practicing shamatha in the rather formless way of now following after thoughts of the past or inviting thoughts about the future, then one should practice shamatha with a support. The most common support, as Rinpoche mentions, is to follow the breath. Five additional supports for the practice of shamatha are mentioned in this text.

If one is still having difficulty achieving the experience of shamatha, then one needs to practice the preliminary practices, or ngondro, to remove karmic obstacles to meditation; to create openness, surrender to the teachings, and proper motivation; to accumulate virtue and positive spiritual energy; and to induce the merging of one's own mind with the enlightened aspect of the guru's mind, thereby drawing into one's mental continuum the blessings of the enlightened state transmitted by the root and lineage gurus.

If one is having difficulty in motivating oneself to practice, one needs to think long and hard about the fundamental truths of samsaric existence as embodied in the "four thoughts that turn the mind to dharma." These are presented here, but if one requires greater detail, one can find them in all books that give a systematic presentation of the path, such as Gampopa's *Jewel Ornament of Liberation* or Jamgon Kongtrul's *Torch of Certainty*. In particular, one needs to evaluate and reevaluate one's own personal samsaric agendas in light of their inevitable consequences as illuminated by these teachings. Just as bodhichitta is the heart of dharma, these four thoughts that turn the mind to dharma are the adrenaline.

If one finds oneself so emotionally conflicted that one dislikes meditation or dislikes what one sees when one meditates, one needs to adopt a policy of meditating at first only for very short periods of time—thirty seconds, forty-five seconds, two minutes, five minutes—and one needs to evaluate one's conduct and one's relationship with others in light of the seven points of mind training as presented, for example, in Jamgon Kongtrul's *Great Path to Awakening*, and in light of the teachings of Shantideva's *Bodhisattvacharya-vatara*, sometimes rendered *Bodhicharyavatara*, or in English, *A Guide to the Bodhisattva's Way of Life* or *The Way of the Bodhisattva*.

The teachings of mahamudra are the essence of all the Buddha's teachings. Together with the teachings of dzogchen, they comprise what is known as the path of liberation. Traditionally, these teachings are practiced in tandem with deity meditation and the various tantric yogas that comprise the stages of creation and completion of the path of means, the path of method. This was not overly difficult to do in the highly spacious and open conditions of Tibet and other Himalayan countries. But in the very busy, highly stimulating, and stressful conditions of Western life, it is often difficult to find the time, the opportunity, the motivation, and even the willingness to practice the path of method. Practiced without the proper foundation and preparation in shamatha and vipashyana, without proper motivation and training in the practice of bodhichitta, without a substantial accumulation of merit and wisdom, and outside of an appropriate environment, some of the advanced practices of the completion stage can actually lead to even greater stress and, as it states clearly in tantric literature, can endanger one's health and sanity.

But the teachings of mahamudra are much gentler, and their practice leads to further and further relaxation and openness, to the gradual resolution and elimination of all personal mental and emotional problems, to increasing mental clarity and intelligence, and to the general well-being and uplifting of sentient existence—and one can still get enlightened practicing them.

I would like to point out that, since Vajrayana regards the enlightened state as the path and not simply as the goal, for these teachings to be truly effective one must receive or have received some introduction to the nature of mind from the tantric tradition, whether that occurs or has occurred in a totally informal situation, in a teaching on mahamudra, or in a tantric ritual such as an empowerment. And it is important that such an introduction be received in the very presence of the lama.

—*Lama Tashi Namgyal*

ACKNOWLEDGMENT

Thrangu Rinpoche's commentary on Pointing Out the Dharmakaya *was given over the course of three periods of teaching in 1995–1997 in British Columbia, Canada. We would like to express our gratitude to Khenchen Thrangu Rinpoche for having given these teachings, and to extend our thanks to Ping Yau and Karme Thekchen Choling of Vancouver, B.C. for having sponsored them.*

1 INTRODUCTION

The Lineage Supplication

I'M DELIGHTED to see that all of you have come here to practice meditation and to practice dharma out of your enthusiasm and devotion, and I would like to thank each and every one of you for doing so. I'd like to begin by reciting the lineage supplication. The particular lineage supplication we use is recited in all of the major seats of the Karma Kagyu lineage, including Tsurphu and Palpung.[1] All Kagyu teachers and all practitioners recite it. The reason we use this particular supplication is that it has a special blessing that is distinct from other similar supplications. It was composed by Penkar Jampal Zangpo,[2] who composed it after spending eighteen years in meditation on mahamudra on an island in the middle of Sky Lake in the north of Tibet. This supplication bears the blessing of his realization of mahamudra during his eighteen years of practice and is considered very profound. When you chant the lineage supplication, imagine that Vajradhara, Tilopa, Naropa, and the rest of the lineage are actually present in the sky in front of you, and with that confidence, supplicate them for the bestowal of their blessings.

Mahamudra Meditation

In general, mahamudra is an approach to meditation and attainment that does not require a great deal of elaboration, either in practice or in the preparation for practice. In the practice of mahamudra, we do not need an elaborate environment, such as utter darkness, nor do we need elaborate practices, such as physical postures. Therefore, I think this practice is especially appropriate and beneficial in this modern age.

The teachings of the Buddha have been classified as sutra and tantra teachings; mahamudra is primarily derived from the tantra or Vajrayana teaching. In particular, the mahamudra teachings derive from such tantras as the *Mahamudra-tilaka-tantra* and the *Glorious Stainless Tantra*. This teaching spread throughout India and was initially propagated by the mahasiddha

Saraha, from whom it has descended in several lineages. Eventually, eighty-four mahasiddhas arose in India who attained realization through the mahamudra practice.

The significance of the eighty-four mahasiddhas is not so much that there were only eighty-four individuals who were able to attain enlightenment, as that these eighty-four individuals were examples of various lifestyles within which we can practice mahamudra successfully. Because the eighty-four mahasiddhas had very different lifestyles, the common factor between them was that they all practiced mahamudra meditation, through which practice they all attained actual realization. The point is that one's particular lifestyle is not that important. For example, one mahasiddha was King Indrabhuti, who, as a king, was very rich and very busy and appeared to be attached to pleasure. Yet, having received the mahamudra instructions, King Indrabhuti practiced according to the instructions while still king, still rich and busy, still having a good time, and he attained the supreme siddhi[3] (enlightenment) through mahamudra practice and thereby became a mahasiddha. The lesson we can draw from this is that even a person who is very rich and very busy can still practice mahamudra properly.

Another example of the mahasiddhas is Nagarjuna, who was a great scholar. He was so brilliant, in fact, that no one could ever successfully argue with him. He composed a large number of commentaries on the Buddha's teachings, and he had an enormous number of students he had to take care of. While busy with all of these activities, he practiced mahamudra, and through doing so he too attained the supreme siddhi.

A further example is Tilopa, whose occupation was principally pounding sesame seeds to produce sesame oil. He was neither rich nor particularly scholarly. While engaged in this manual occupation and the even more menial occupation of being a servant, living in a simple but somewhat austere manner, he practiced mahamudra, and he too attained the supreme siddhi. The lesson we draw from his life is that we can practice mahamudra successfully and attain the supreme siddhi even while having to do menial work.

In the same way, some of the mahasiddhas were street cleaners, some smiths, some weavers, some shoemakers, some tailors, and some were kings. They had a variety of lifestyles and a variety of occupations. The only thing they all had in common was that they all practiced mahamudra meditation and thereby all attained the supreme siddhi. The lesson we can draw from all these examples is that whether or not we have great responsibilities to fulfill, whether or not we are very busy, whether or not we are rich, whether or not we are scholars, whether or not we do menial labor, whether we are female or male: none of these things has any bearing on the practice of mahamudra.

Under any circumstance, we can always practice mahamudra, and we can attain the supreme siddhi.

When the mahamudra teachings were first brought to Tibet, they were propagated initially by three individuals whom we regard as the three great progenitors of the Kagyu tradition: Marpa, Milarepa, and Gampopa. Marpa was a householder with a wife, a number of sons, a great deal of property, and many disciples he had to teach and take care of. Yet, in the midst of all these entanglements and responsibilities, he was able to go to India under conditions of the utmost hardship, meet many of the great mahasiddhas, and receive instruction from them, particularly the mahamudra, which he practiced and thereby attained the supreme siddhi. So he was able to practice successfully and attain the result while being wealthy and surrounded by his family and responsibilities.

The second of these three great teachers was Milarepa, whose lifestyle was utterly different from that of his teacher, Marpa. His entire life was devoted to practice under conditions of the utmost privation and simplicity. He lived in caves because they provided shelter without having to be built, and he practiced meditation continually, whether he had food or not. His lifestyle of complete renunciation led to his attainment of the supreme siddhi, just as Marpa's lifestyle had led to his attainment. For some people, Milarepa's lifestyle is an appropriate one in which to practice mahamudra and attain the supreme siddhi.

The third teacher was Milarepa's student Gampopa, whose lifestyle was different from either of his predecessors. Gampopa took the monastic ordination, met his teacher Milarepa, from whom he received the instructions of mahamudra, and practiced these instructions while living as a monk. Later, in accordance with Milarepa's instructions, he established a monastery, which he looked after as abbot for the rest of his life. He taught and took care of many disciples, and while meditating under these circumstances, he too fully realized mahamudra and attained the supreme siddhi. Having done so, he taught a vast number of students. From Gampopa's lifestyle, we can observe that one can also practice mahamudra as a monastic.

Like lifestyle, it makes no difference whether you are female or male. As the Buddha said in the *Heart Sutra*: "A son or daughter of noble family who wishes to meditate upon the Prajnaparamita ..." That statement of the Buddha has the significance of pointing out that it makes no difference whether a practitioner is male or female. What makes a difference in reaching enlightenment is the degree to which one is motivated, the degree to which one wishes to realize mahamudra, the intensity of one's faith and diligence.

In general, the practice of mahamudra is essential for any practitioner of dharma, but in my experience and my judgment, mahamudra is especially appropriate for Westerners and other persons living in modern society. Nowadays many people wish to practice, and their enthusiasm is genuine. They want to meditate, and yet the lifestyle of a simple renunciant, which used to seem like the most sensible lifestyle for a practitioner, simply does not fit in with contemporary society. For example, in earlier times, it was possible for a practitioner to survive by begging for food. Nowadays begging for food is difficult; people have to work to take care of their life needs. Dharma practitioners frequently think that, by taking care of the needs of this life, they are wasting their life and, therefore, failing as a practitioner. In fact, this sense of failure is unnecessary. You need to take care of yourself in this life, but while fulfilling your responsibilities, you can still take care of your mind, and you can still practice meditation. This does not require any dramatic change in lifestyle, such as extreme external renunciation.

Now, if you choose great austerity, you can devote years of your life to retreat, which is excellent. But even if you can't do that, you can still practice mahamudra very effectively by devoting what time you can to it in the midst of a life filled with occupation and responsibility. So this is a path that is extremely simple, meaning that it does not require a lot of preparation or devices, and so can be practiced at any time or in any situation, provided one possesses mindfulness and alertness. So it is exactly this that needs to be practiced by monastics; they can practice just this mahamudra without having to add anything to it or search for anything more profound, and they will accomplish liberation. And it is just this that can be practiced by male and female householders; they need not add anything else to this or look for anything more profound, in order to accomplish liberation.

The root of mahamudra practice is the maintenance of mindfulness and alertness in your mind, which needs to be cultivated, both in formal meditation practice and in post-meditation. The post-meditation discipline of maintaining mindfulness and alertness in the midst of one's activities, such as walking, sitting, talking, eating, and so on, is rather difficult for beginners. But if you keep on practicing this discipline without becoming discouraged, it becomes not too difficult, and you can actually accomplish liberation of your mind, which is why mahamudra is called the path of liberation, which is simple or free of elaboration.

In addition to the path of liberation, there is within the Kagyu tradition another path or instruction for practice, called the path of method or upaya, which refers to the *Six Dharmas of Naropa*. If you practice the mahamudra path of liberation diligently, then through that you can accomplish the ultimate result. If you practice the path of upaya, the Six Dharmas of Naropa, with diligence, through that as well you can accomplish the ultimate result. However, between these two aspects of our tradition, that on which we place primary emphasis is mahamudra, the path of liberation. Essentially, therefore, this path is sufficient in and of itself. On the other hand, it is appropriate to enhance one's training of the view and meditation of mahamudra with such supplementary practices as the creation stage of yidam practice, the practice of guru yoga, the practices of the path of upaya, such as the Six Dharmas of Naropa, and other practices that involve conceptual effort. All of these practices are helpful to mahamudra and not harmful to it. Therefore, it is the custom, when we have the time and opportunity, to engage in these elaborate practices, even up to the preparation of mandalas, the making and offering of tormas, and so on. If these practices are done with a proper meditation, or samadhi, and clear visualization, and so forth, then they can bestow great benefit or enhancement upon one's fundamental mahamudra practice.

Sometimes the supplementary practices you do need not be too elaborate. They could be simpler practices, such as the meditations on Chenrezig, Amitabha, Medicine Buddha, and so forth. All of these practices can be used as contexts for the practice of mahamudra and all of them are helpful. You should not think that in order to supplement your mahamudra practice you need necessarily to do very complicated and elaborate practices. Whatever type of practice you do, if you mix it with the mahamudra practice, it will facilitate that practice.

Mahamudra and Dzogchen[4]

Two different lineages of the meditation of looking directly at mind arose in the Vajrayana in Tibet. One was the mahamudra and the other was the dzogchen lineage. Different teachers have made somewhat different statements about the relationship between these two styles of practice and teaching. Some have said that dzogchen is more profound than mahamudra; others have said that mahamudra is more profound than dzogchen; but most have said that they are the same thing. The instructions in both of these traditions is simply called "guidance on the mind" because in both systems everything hinges on the student's recognition of the nature of mind. By looking at texts from both systems, one finds that they point to the same thing. In fact, in many cases they use the same words. In his *Aspiration Prayer for Mahamudra,* the Third Karmapa, Rangjung Dorje, says:

This freedom from mental directedness is mahamudra;
This freedom from extremes is the great middle way;

As it includes everything, this is the great perfection (dzogchen).
May I have the confidence that realizing one is understanding
   them all.

Further in the text, he says:

It does not exist and has not been seen by any of the victorious ones.
It does not not exist; it is the basis of samsara and nirvana.
It is not a contradiction; it is the middle way of unity.
May I recognize this dharmata of the mind.

From the dzogchen tradition, a text from Jigme Lingpa reads:

It does not exist and has not been seen by any of the victorious ones.
It does not not exist; it is the basis of samsara and nirvana.
It is not a contradiction but is beyond expression.
May I realize dzogchen, the ground of all things.

Wangchuk Dorje's Text

In the times of Tilopa, Naropa, Marpa, and Milarepa, the format of maha-mudra instructions was primarily brief spiritual songs of instruction called dohas that were quite spontaneous. These were given to a disciple who would meditate upon the instruction and then return to the teacher and describe his or her experience. On the basis of the student's experiences, the teacher would give further instruction as needed. Through this process of exchange and experiential oral instruction, the disciple or student would attain realization and then would train his own students in the same way. In that way, the mahamudra lineage was initially one of oral instruction, called an oral lineage or heard lineage. This type of instruction is very pro-found and effective. However, as time went on, there were more and more practitioners, more disciples, requiring a more systematized format of instruction. Also, as time went on, disciples became less diligent in engag-ing in this process, so it became necessary to write down these instructions that had been transmitted. In the Kagyu tradition, the writing down of the oral instructions happened primarily during the time of the Ninth Kar-mapa, Wangchuk Dorje, who lived in the fifteenth century. He wrote three main expositions of mahamudra practice: the longest of these is called *The Ocean of Definitive Meaning* (Tib. *Ngedon Gyamtso*), the medium length text is called *Dispelling the Darkness of Ignorance* (Tib. *Ma rig Munsel*), and the briefest one, this text, is *Pointing Out the Dharmakaya* (Tib. *Choku Dzuptsuk*).

While it is true that the longest of the three texts, *The Ocean of Definitive Meaning*, is quite vast and that *Pointing Out the Dharmakaya* is the shortest of the three, this (latter) text still gives a full treatment of mahamudra practice. This book has several sections. The first part of the text is devoted to the four preliminaries of mahamudra practice, and the bulk of the text describes the actual practice, divided into the practice of tranquility meditation (Skt. *shamatha*, Tib. *shinay*) and the practice of insight meditation (Skt. *vipashyana*, Tib. *lhag tong*).[5] In the section on tranquility meditation, a variety of methods are outlined. In the section on insight, a variety of methods for practicing the insight aspect of mahamudra are also given.

The style of the text is indicated by its name, *Pointing Out the Dharmakaya*, describing the way the text is to be used. Because of its brevity, the text is a convenient practical manual for mahamudra practitioners. It is easy to use, and it is easy to keep the instructions in mind. The instructions enable the practitioner to get directly at the nature of his or her mind.

The Importance of Devotion

Throughout *Pointing Out the Dharmakaya*, the point is made again and again, and this is the same point that is made in one of the stanzas of the Kagyu lineage supplication. In the lineage supplication, we recite, "Devotion is the head of meditation," the point being that the most important element in the practice of mahamudra is your faith and commitment. As I said before, the lineage supplication by Penkar Jampal Zangpo is an expression of his realization after years of mahamudra practice, and therefore, everything he wrote in that supplication has great meaning. "Devotion is the head of meditation" is a metaphor on many levels. Generally speaking, your head is a very important part of your body because if you have a head, you can see, you can hear, you can talk, you can eat. It is the location of most of the senses. Even though the head is not large compared to the rest of the body, if you don't have a head, your functions are useless.

The relationship of devotion to the rest of meditation is very much like the relationship between your head and the rest of your body. The most important thing that makes meditation work and fruitful is your devotion and commitment.

What we must direct our devotion and commitment toward is the dharma. In this context, when we say "dharma," we mean mahamudra. Devotion and commitment mean having the feeling: "I must meditate on this. If I meditate on this, there will be benefit. These are the actual methods, and they will lead to the goal I wish to achieve."

In short, it is confidence in the validity and efficacy of the mahamudra teachings and practices. It is a trust that, through correctly implementing the instructions we have received from the root guru through the lineage gurus, the attainment of our goal will actually come about. The reason this is so important is that, if we have this commitment based on confidence, then we will naturally be diligent, and if we are diligent, then we will get results.

Motivation for Practice

Whether one is practicing dharma in the form of meditation or one is listening to dharma, it is important that one's motivation for doing so be unlimited. While practicing and studying mahamudra, one is concerned with the practice of meditation. If in this study and practice one's concern is for one's own benefit alone, the result will not be complete or perfect, because the motivation is insufficient. In order to study and practice properly you need to have as your motivation the thought that you are working to attain Buddhahood in order to be able to liberate all beings. "All beings" means all beings, without exception, who fill space. In order to attain Buddhahood you must practice the path of meditation. If with that motivation of bodhichitta you meditate or listen to the dharma, then great benefit will ensue. On the other hand, if you practice or study without the altruistic motivation of bodhichitta, then because of the limited quality or pettiness of your motivation, the practice will not function properly. Therefore, when you set about practicing or studying any aspect of Vajrayana, such as mahamudra, or dzogchen, it is necessary that you generate in your mind the motivation of bodhichitta.

While we generally think of bodhichitta as being an attitude of love or compassion, in fact, to be authentic bodhichitta, it must have two aspects or characteristics. The first is the aspect of compassion, which is altruism. This altruism, which is a deep concern for the benefit of others, must be unlimited, in that it must be directed to all beings equally. After all, one has had intimate family connections—as mother, father, and children—throughout innumerable previous lives with all beings. The basic attitude of the compassion aspect of bodhichitta is that, recognizing that all beings wish to be free from the sufferings of samsara but do not know how to free themselves from these sufferings, you must protect and free them yourself.

The second aspect or characteristic of bodhichitta is prajna[6] or knowledge that is focused on perfect awakening. This means that your intention to free all beings is not limited to the idea of freeing them merely from their present sufferings but from all of the sufferings of samsara. Therefore, through prajna, your wish to benefit beings is focused on bringing all beings to the completely awakened state of Buddhahood. So, whenever you practice or study mahamudra, and when you receive teachings on it, please do so with this special intention. Please think, "I am studying and practicing this in order to bring all beings to a state of complete freedom from samsara." Please try to remember this [twofold motivation of bodhichitta] in every session as well as when you practice, because it will cause your practice and study to be of much greater benefit.

2 THE PRELIMINARIES

The General Preliminaries

WHEN THE DHARMA spread to Tibet it was practiced in the context of the "secret mantra Vajrayana."[7] The way in which the Four Noble Truths were practiced in the Vajrayana was by way of what are known as the "four thoughts that turn the mind." These are (1) the difficulty of finding a free and well-favoured situation,[8] (2) death and impermanence, (3) karma and its effects, and (4) the disadvantages of cyclic existence (Skt. *samsara*).

Taking these a little out of order:

The Contemplation of Impermanence

The main thought which turns the mind away from samsara is impermanence. The Buddha said that the nature of samsara is suffering. Learned persons and great practitioners of the past have studied this teaching of impermanence carefully. They found that when one doesn't recognize impermanent things as being impermanent, then one will become attached to various appearances of samsara which seem to create happiness, but really don't. Being influenced by attachment to impermanent things makes it so we cannot enter the dharma. Not being able to enter the dharma means we won't practice and will never alleviate our suffering.

Fundamentally, the contemplation on impermanence is the recollection of the fact that everything in the universe, including every being, is in a state of constant change.

Many persons think that the Buddhist way is not good because it believes that impermanence leads to negativity such as saying everything is emptiness. However, in fact, there is an important reason for stressing impermanence at the very beginning of the path.

The reason impermanence and selflessness are taught from the beginning is that these are the actual characteristics of things or phenomena. Even though impermanence is a characteristic of samsara we tend to not actually notice and understand its actual character. For this reason the Buddha said, "Through recognizing the actual nature of phenomena in samsara, we will be able to achieve the great kingdom."

Let us illustrate this with an ordinary example. Suppose there were a poisonous snake right next to where I am sitting and I didn't know about it. As long as I didn't know about it, I am sitting here comfortably and happily while there is a great danger that I am not aware of. Gradually this poisonous snake comes closer and closer and then it bites me. After it does so I find myself in a very difficult situation, with a lot of pain and hardship, in fact, I am helpless. If, on the other hand someone were to say to me, "There is a poisonous snake right near where you are," even though that might be a bit alarming and painful to hear right then, nevertheless, it would allow me to escape from the danger and not undergo the hardship of being bitten. For this reason, the Buddha and the spiritual friends of the past taught initially that impermanence and suffering are the nature of phenomena of samsara, so that it is possible to turn away from and to flee from that. So, there is a real reason in teaching impermanence.

The Difficulty of Finding a Free and Well-Favored Birth

Impermanence is the definitive mark of samsara and if we consider the lifetime of human beings, we see that the lifetime of human beings is short. For instance, there are some turtles that live to be three or four hundred years old. Human beings don't live to be three hundred years old, so from that point of view, the lifetime of human beings is very short. In that short lifetime, it is extremely important to practice the dharma so we can pass beyond the impermanent things of samsara. Is it possible for us to cross over this ocean of samsara to the far shore and achieve freedom from impermanent, painful conditions? Well, if we were talking about animals or hungry ghosts, it is almost impossible for them to reach enlightenment. However, our situation is that we have the very good fortune of having the body of a human being, with which we are able to practice the dharma of the Buddha. We have the intelligence which makes it possible for us to understand those things that are to be done and those things that are to be discarded. It is from this point of view that the teachers of the past have said that having a human body is extremely fortunate and is extremely difficult to attain. Receiving a human body is extremely important and fortunate. It is the basis for liberation from samsara; a state of complete freedom.

The Contemplation of the Retribution of Samsara

So, when we have a human body what is the method for achieving liberation from samsara? How then shall we practice? Shall we focus upon achieving the happiness that is included within samsara by abandoning the unpleasant and painful situations of samsara? No, the happiness of samsara is not very stable and the happiness and pleasure we need is something beyond temporary happiness, that is other than the happiness within samsara. So the learned and accomplished persons of the past have talked about the unsatisfying, faulty nature of samsara, saying even the pleasures of samsara are temporary and have no lasting benefit or meaning.

The Contemplation of Karma and Its Result

Is it possible to abandon the suffering of samsara and pass beyond the suffering of samsara? If the world were created by a god then we would be helpless. It would not be within our own power to do much about our own situation, and achieve real happiness. However, some deity has not created the world, so we have the power to do something about our situation. That is because the situation we are in is the fruition of our own actions; our actions are a cause that has created this particular effect. Therefore it is within our power to abandon the causes of suffering. For instance, we hear about the great suffering that beings have to undergo in the lower realms and we feel frightened by that and do not want to have to experience that kind of suffering. So, is it within our own power to prevent the experience of this kind of suffering? Yes, it is because ill deeds and non-virtuous activities are the causes of being born in a lower realm. And it is within our power not to engage in such ill deeds and unfavourable activities. If, on the other hand, we wish to enjoy the happiness of the higher realms within samsara, we can do that because the practice of virtuous actions is the cause of taking birth in a comfortable, pleasant and good situation; a high migration within cyclic existence (samsara). In that way, it is within our own power to do what we want to do. If we want to achieve nirvana or the state of having crossed beyond all suffering of cyclic existence we can simply engage in the causes that lead to nirvana.

The Buddha initially explained the Four Noble Truths and in particular the truth of suffering. As I said before, in Tibet where the tradition of the Vajrayana was most widely practiced,[9] this teaching on suffering was practiced mainly in terms of the four thoughts that turns one's mind from samsara. These were practiced first of all through understanding these four points.

Having understood them, we then meditate upon them by making it extremely clear and vivid in our mind and doing this again and again and again, until we have become extremely accustomed and familiar with it, to the point in which it actually dwells in our mind and we have a great confidence in it.

The Four Special Preliminaries

THE INSTRUCTION OF TAKING REFUGE AND AROUSING BODHICHITTA

We should first understand what it really means to take refuge, what the purpose of refuge is, and the benefits we can expect from taking refuge. Ordinarily when we encounter pain, suffering, or fear, we wonder where we can look for protection against these. Sometimes we will look for comfort from our parents. Or we will look for this in worldly affairs. But these are not the answer because they can only help us for a short time.

Only the three jewels of the Buddha, the dharma, and the sangha can protect us from pain and help us gain liberation. They are the only things that can really protect us and they can help us in ways other things cannot. The reason other beings cannot help us avoid suffering and truly protect us is that they themselves have no control over their own suffering and have not reached liberation themselves. So only the three jewels are in a position to truly help us. This is why we take refuge in the Buddha, the dharma, and the sangha.

But how do we take refuge in three jewels? Do we think of them as the ones who can give us liberation and cure our suffering? No, we cannot expect them to do this for us because our liberation depends on us. We do, however, need someone to show us the way; that being the Buddha who is our guide. We need a path and this is the dharma. We also need friends to help us on the path and this is the sangha.

To this three-fold general refuge there are three more refuges in the Vajrayana tradition. These are known as the three roots. The first root is the lama or guru who is the root of blessing. He or she is the one who shows us the path and gives us blessing.[10] The Buddha can do this, but we can not meet the Buddha so we have to rely on the lama to do that for us. We are able to meet a root guru and receive the teachings from him or her. So, as far as we are concerned, all of the Buddha's teachings and all his blessings come to us through the root guru. He has the power to give us this and this is why we take refuge in the lama as the root of blessing in the Vajrayana.

The second root of the refuge is the root of spiritual accomplishments, which is the yidam. In general, we take refuge in the dharma as being the path through which we can achieve the ultimate fruition and in this way accomplish all the positive qualities. In the profound Vajrayana practice we take refuge in the dharma and we practice the dharma, but we do this in a particular form by practicing yidam meditation. We practice yidam meditation both in the creation stage and the completion stage. Through this our ability to meditate gradually increases and becomes better and better.

With yidam practice we will be able to achieve the ordinary spiritual accomplishments which are qualities such as clairvoyance and various forms of deeper understanding in the short term. In the long term, we will be able to achieve the supreme spiritual accomplishment, which is Buddhahood. So the yidam can help us achieve the ultimate fruition. Outwardly, taking refuge in the yidam means we choose to commit ourself to that particular practice. Once we've committed ourself to that, we are going to work on it until it brings us to the ultimate goal of enlightenment. This is why we take refuge in the yidam in the Vajrayana.

The third root of refuge is the root of activity that corresponds to the dharma protectors, the dakas, and the dakinis. Generally, we take refuge in the sangha as our companions on the path. These companions are important because they are the ones who help us follow the path correctly. They can stop us from falling into an incorrect path and thus remove the obstacles that might arise on our path. If we become too involved with pleasures, or meet with difficult circumstances, they can help us to avoid these difficulties in practice. They therefore make it easier for us to follow the true path.

The special aspect of the sangha is the dharma protectors, dakas, and dakinis. We cannot see them directly, but they are the ones who can remove those subtle obstacles that might interrupt our life prematurely or cause difficulties for our body and mind. They can also eliminate obstacles that would interrupt our dharma activity. So in the Vajrayana they constitute one aspect of the sangha and we therefore take refuge in the protectors and dakas and dakinis as the root of Buddha activity.

All the refuges are included in the three jewels and the three roots. But one could say that all these aspects are already contained in the three jewels in the form of the teacher, the path, and the companions. The objects of refuge give us the blessings, the spiritual accomplishments, and remove the obstacles. But we could also say that all these various aspects are contained within the guru (Tib. *lama*). The lama, after all, is the one who can perform these functions for us. So it is said that the guru embodies all the aspects of the refuge.

In summary, we can say there are six sources of refuge, but more concisely that there are three sources of refuge or still more concisely there is one refuge, the guru, who embodies all the other aspects. A more detailed explanation of refuge can be found in Gampopa's *Jewel Ornament of Liberation* which has a very full explanation of the purpose of refuge, the source of refuge, and the benefits of practice that come from taking refuge.

The taking of refuge in prostration practice involves creating the following visualization while reciting, "In front of me is a lake and in the middle of the lake is the great wish-fulfilling tree...."[11] So we imagine all the things that are described in this recitation and take refuge in the six sources of refuge. In the center is the root guru and then in the east, west, south, north and below are the five other aspects of refuge. We take refuge physically, verbally, and mentally. Physically we do prostrations, verbally we recite the refuge prayer, and mentally we visualize the refuge tree. We also develop the three aspects of faith: the faith of listening, the faith of aspiration, and the faith of confidence. We pray that all the aspects of refuge which are the body, speech, mind, quality, and action of the Buddha will be born in us. So with this confidence we take refuge in the six aspects of refuge.

Taking refuge is immediately followed by the taking of the vow of bodhichitta. We generate the wish to reach Buddhahood for the sake of all beings.[12] We think that whatever we are going to do, whether it is the taking of refuge or any subsequent practice, we will do it to reach Buddhahood for the purpose of helping all other beings reach enlightenment. So the second aspect of this practice is the resolution to reach enlightenment for the sake of all beings. The text says, "Just as the Buddhas of the past first generated bodhichitta and progressed stage by stage through the different levels of the bodhisattva training, so in the same way, I also generate the bodhichitta for the good of all beings. I will also progressively practice that same training." This means that we are following the examples of all the Buddhas of the past who at one time set their mind on reaching perfect enlightenment for the sake of all beings. Similarly, we are making the same commitment by going through the five paths of accumulation, junction, insight, cultivation, and accomplishment, (Buddhahood). At each of these levels the Buddhas did certain practices, behaved in a certain way, and performed certain actions to accomplish enlightenment for the sake of other beings. When we make this same commitment, we think that from today onwards we are going to try to act in the same way as all the Buddhas did to accomplish enlightenment. Once this is done all our actions become a cause for enlightenment. This is why we take the bodhisattva vow every day after we have taken refuge, to renew this commitment.

After the bodhisattva vow we say, "Now my life is fruitful. I have obtained a precious human existence. I rejoice." Why do we rejoice? We rejoice because we have taken refuge and made a commitment to reach Buddhahood for the sake of all beings. Once we have done this, everything we do becomes meaningful. We know that all our actions are beneficial, deeply meaningful, and once we have acknowledged this, we rejoice.

Why is it important to rejoice? If we do not really appreciate the value of what we are doing and are not happy about it, then we may regret having taken the bodhisattva commitment when difficulties arise. If we are not really aware of the goodness of what we are doing then when difficulties arise, little by little our enthusiasm for the practice, our faith, and our diligence will decrease. However, if we rejoice in the goodness of what we are doing, we will be aware of just how valuable our practice is and we will be very happy. Once we are in this state of mind, then whatever we are doing can only get better. We will want to do it more and more. It is not suitable to regret good things that we have done, or good things we are about to do. So the importance of rejoicing is that it will reinforce our interest in the practice and our desire to practice.

We should also invite other beings to rejoice in what we are doing. We are taking this commitment not on our own but in front of all the Buddhas and bodhisattvas, deities, great sages, and realized beings. So we are asking them to witness our oath. They are witnessing this so that once we have taken this promise, we know that we can't go back on it. We have to keep the promise very carefully and it would be really negative to go against it. That is why we take this oath in the presence of so many witnesses in the practice.

The Practice of Vajrasattva

We begin Vajrasattva (Tib. *Dorje Sempa*) practice with the Kagyu lineage prayer. Immediately after that, we do the four general preliminary practices; contemplating the four topics that turn the mind away from samsara (precious human birth, impermanence, karma, and the faults of samsara). After that we do the refuge prayer and recitation. Then we resolve to reach enlightenment for the sake of all sentient beings. As we are doing the preliminary practices we try to think of the meaning of what we are reciting, and try to do all the correct visualizations as we go along.

In the Vajrasattva practice we take refuge to increase our faith and try to transform out faith into the kind of faith which is unshakable in the face of desire, anger, or stupidity. This is why we think again and again of refuge so that we develop irreversible faith and total confidence in the three jewels (the Buddha, the dharma, and the sangha). By doing this practice every day, our faith, and our confidence in the three jewels becomes clearer and more and more stable. Because there are many different paths it is very possible to stray into a mistaken one. It is said that refuge constitutes the protection against straying onto the wrong path. When we take refuge, it helps us follow the path of the Buddha properly. Taking refuge will help us to go on the correct path all the way to Buddhahood without getting lost on the way.

We next generate enlightened heart or bodhichitta by committing ourselves to reaching enlightenment for the sake of all beings. It is said that this is a protection against falling into a lower path. We can follow the narrow path (Hinayana) of self-realization or the greater path of the Mahayana. By engendering bodhichitta we can avoid falling into the Hinayana path and follow the great path of the Mahayana. This is why we practice taking refuge and why we resolve to reach enlightenment for the sake of all beings. We do this again and again, so that we can follow the right path.

The goal of all practice is accomplishing Buddhahood. To accomplish Buddhahood, we need to develop genuine meditation which is the goal of all Buddhist teachings.

The *Uttaratantra* by the Maitreya Buddha, for example, is divided into seven different vajra topics; the first three are about the three jewels, the fourth is about the Buddha essence, with the fifth about the qualities of enlightenment and the sixth about Buddha activity. The purpose of the *Uttaratantra* is to show us how all these enlightened qualities can be developed so that we can reach a point where true meditation can really arise in us. Gampopa's *Jewel Ornament of Liberation* begins with the four thoughts that turn the mind and then discusses refuge. Next it talks about bodhichitta, the way to develop the wish to reach enlightenment for the sake of all beings. By studying these topics carefully we gradually begin to understand the Prajnaparamita which makes it possible to develop the insight into the true nature of phenomena (Skt. *dharmata*) when we can achieve true meditation.

The four preliminary practices (Tib. *ngondro*) have the same underlying goal. They are intended to lead us to a point where we can develop true meditation. Although they have the same goal, they go at achieving realization in different ways using different tools. Some teachings help us acquire knowledge and develop a conviction of the truth of the teachings so we are able to work on the path and eventually realize this through meditation. Other teachings are based on the purification of obscurations that will automatically free us for pure meditation.

We've seen how we take refuge and how we could turn our mind to enlightenment for the sake of all beings. But now we have to develop true meditation. We cannot simply do true meditation, because, we will meet obstacles that will hinder our meditation. These obstacles come from all our harmful deeds that we have accumulated from all our past lives. Since beginningless time, we have acted in a negative way and the fruition of this is many obstacles to our practice that makes meditation difficult. We will also encounter obscurations that are the result of our previous negative habits and these create emotional obscurations and cognitive obscurations. These previous actions create a very thick ignorance, which prevents us from seeing the true nature of phenomena and preventing us from having clarity in our meditation. These obstacles continually disrupt our shamatha and vipashyana meditation by producing many thoughts and mental agitation. This is why we need to purify these impurities which are our harmful deeds and obscurations. If we can purify these, then our meditation will automatically increase and become clear and stable. The best way that we can do this is with the Vajrayana practice of Vajrasattva, which involves reciting the hundred-syllable Vajrasattva mantra.

The Vajrasattva practice is the second preliminary practice, but it is also by itself a very exceptional practice because it is very profound and it brings about many great benefits. Vajrasattva practice is beneficial because we as human beings all want to avoid pain and suffering at all costs. We don't want to suffer physically or mentally and we all want to find happiness. To attain happiness we must first acknowledge that suffering is not going to go away by itself. Happiness will not occur automatically because it is the effect of our previous actions. If we have acted in a negative way in the past, we will experience suffering now. And if we haven't generated any virtuous actions in the past, then we haven't created any causal condition for happiness to be present in our present circumstances. So even though we might be thinking, "I want happiness" if we have not planted the seed of happiness with our previous actions, there will be no way in which we can experience happiness now. Also if we have created a causal condition for suffering with a negative action before, then there is no way one can avoid that suffering presently.

There is however, a way out of this cycle. Before we entered the path of dharma, we didn't pay very much attention to our actions and so out of carelessness we acted in a very unskillful and unwholesome way. However, once we enter the path of dharma, we can become much more attentive to our actions and we can try to avoid doing negative things. But from time to time we will be overpowered by our desire, our anger, our jealously and so on and this will lead us into acting in a non-virtuous way.

Even though we are practicing good Buddhist conduct, from time to time we will still do some of the ten non-virtuous actions,[13] or we may even do one of the five actions which brings an immediate result at death.[14] This happens because we are not in full control of our mind yet. The Buddha said that it is not the earth, or the mountains, or the trees, which will experience the fruition of their actions. It is sentient beings who do. Whoever acts in a certain way, has to experience the results of their own actions. So we have to understand that it is quite important for us to stop the source of suffering, because the suffering which results from our negative actions will bring very painful results.

If we do slip and do a negative action, we have to try and prevent our negative actions from coming to fruition. The way we can stop this is to purify all our negative actions [15] If our negative actions mature, we will experience many obstacles, difficulties, sickness, and other unfavourable circumstances. Because of this purifying impurities is especially important for our next life, because unpurified negative deeds might ripen into suffering in the three lower realms. Purification is also very important for our dharma practice because as long as we possess negative karma there will be great impediments to our practice. The best way to purify these previous negative actions is through Vajrasattva meditation and the recitation of his mantra.

At one time or another we have also enjoyed great happiness when everything seems to be going right. We might become lost in this pleasure and forget that we need to practice the dharma. This is a bad mistake because this temporal kind of happiness will not go on forever. Because we had some positive karma in the past, we will experience some happiness now; but because we also have negative karma, we will also experience suffering again. So even if happiness comes, we must remember that we want to stop the flow of suffering altogether though purification, and the best way to do this is the Vajrasattva practice and the recitation of his mantra.

In the preliminary practice of Vajrasattva we recite 111,000 Vajrasattva mantras. When we do this practice, we must not just focus on the idea of doing as many mantras as possible. The mantras should be recited correctly. When doing this meditation, our body should be in meditation posture; straight and firm. We should recite the hundred-syllable mantra with it being just audible, but not distorted. Our mind should focus clearly on the visualization of Vajrasattva and on the flow of healing nectar (Skt. *amrita*) into us.[16] Visualizing should be done as clearly as we can without distraction. From time to time in our meditation we can think that whatever suffering we are experiencing is the result of our negative karma and we should have a very strong desire to purify it. We should very sincerely repent our negative actions and regret them and we should also feel very great confidence in the fact that this Vajrasattva meditation can truly purify us. So we remember the four powers of purification[17] and then do the meditation as correctly and sincerely as we can.

If we practice this way then our practice will definitely bear fruit, all our unskilful actions will be purified and there will be the signs of purification. But if we practice in a very casual way, just saying the words and letting our mind wander all over the place, we will derive only a small benefit. Because the mantra has its own value we will derive some benefit from mindlessly repeating the mantra, but we won't derive the full benefit of the practice. So it is important to do the practice properly with as much concentration as we can muster.

A high lama cannot say, "Well, I'm a great bodhisattva and I can give you this practice so that you won't have any more suffering. I can give you enlightenment and you never need to suffer ever again." He or she cannot say this because that would be a lie. What the lama can say is that there is this Vajrasattva practice of purification and if this practice is done properly, it can truly free us from all our impurities and bring about the ultimate realization of Buddhahood.

We are all very fortunate because we can learn about these teachings and then practice them. This is a very great opportunity because everything is impermanent, and there are always so many things to do in our worldly life. So we should take advantage of this precious life of ours as much as we can to achieve our purpose and to fulfil our goals to purify ourselves.

The Instruction on the Mandala Practice

If we do the Vajrasattva practice properly, all our impurities and obscurations will be removed and we will see the signs of this purification in us. We will see that our understanding is sharper, that our meditation is becoming clearer, and that our faith and devotion is increasing. Vajrasattva is a practice that removes the obstacles which are within us and these are all the impurities that are present in us. For meditation to develop properly we need to develop the direct causal condition for meditation which is the presence of a great amount of virtue and meritorious actions. According to the teachings of the sutras, the accumulation of this merit is done mainly through the practice of the six paramitas and takes eons to accomplish. In the Vajrayana, however, we develop this great virtue through the practice of mandala offering. This practice is easy to do and brings about great fruition. In this practice we mentally offer all the various beautiful things in the world to the Buddhas and bodhisattvas. Making this offering doesn't mean the Buddhas and bodhisattvas will be pleased with what we offer them and in return give us what we seek. Rather, making offerings to the Buddhas and bodhisattvas means that when we place our mind in the disposition of making offerings to the Buddhas and bodhisattvas, this disposition fulfills our accumulation of virtue. So this practice is very easy to do and is a way to achieve a great accumulation of virtue very quickly.

The purpose of the preliminary practices is to achieve the realization of mahamudra because realizing mahamudra will liberate us from samsara. What makes it possible for us to have the realization of mahamudra is the presence of a very great amount of virtue and meritorious deeds. This accumulation of merit is like the very strong positive energy that makes it possible for us to enter the dharma properly and not be hindered by obstacles that come up in our practice. Also accumulation of merit makes it possible for true meditation to gradually arise in us. If we were to try to practice without a great amount of virtue to support us, we would find that our practice is weak so that we stop practicing after some time or when obstacles arise. We need the support of this positive energy that comes from accumulated merit so that we can gain the realization of mahamudra. The best way to accumulate merit quickly is through mandala practice.

In mandala practice we imagine that we offer the whole universe to our guru and to the other precious beings. Through this offering we generate a very great amount of virtue which provides us with an accumulation of positive energy that we need for meditation to grow in us. So this accumulation is called "the accumulation of conceptual reference" which means that we still have this accumulation with reference to ourselves.

The other accumulation is the accumulation of the natural insight of dharmata which is free from the dualistic concept of I and other. This non-conceptual accumulation means that whenever we make an offering there is no longer any subject, object, or action of offering. So we no longer possess any concept of someone making the offerings (ourselves), someone receiving offerings (the Buddhas and bodhisattvas), and the offerings being made. When we are able to offer the true nature without any more conceptual separations, we have achieved the second level of the accumulation of wisdom.

At the end of the [mandala] practice we say that through the goodness of having offered the whole of the universe to our guru and to all the precious ones [visualized in front of us], we think that our own accumulations and those of all the other beings have become perfected. Once we've repeated this, we visualize that everything dissolves into light, the light then enters into us, and we become one with that accumulation.

The Guru Yoga That Quickly Brings Blessings

To develop true meditation we must have proper realization. To achieve this realization we need to purify all our harmful actions, impurities, and obscu-

rations. To do this we practice Vajrasattva meditation. If we do this meditation and recite the mantra with genuine regret for all our wrong actions, we
will be purified of not only the unskilful actions and impurities that we have
done, but we will also purify of all the habitual patterns and very fine traces
(Tib. *bag chaks*)[18] that have been left since beginningless time that we have
been in samsara. So all these can be purified by proper practice of Vajrasattva.

Once we have done this purification, we need to work on the direct cause
for realizing meditation. This direct cause is the accumulation of a great
amount of virtue, of positive spiritual energy that will make it possible for us
to develop complete understanding. If we don't have a seed, we won't have a
flower. In the same way, if there is no causal condition for the meditation to
grow, it will not grow. This is why we need to gather the accumulation of
virtue. This has to be done by means of body, speech, and mind. This usually is done through the practice of the six paramitas. But on the special path
of the Vajrayana, there is a very special way to do this by means of the offering of the mandala. This is the very best way to gather a very great amount
of virtue very quickly.

Once we have done mandala practice; we then need something that will
make our understanding and meditation progress quickly and this is the
practice of guru yoga. If we pray to our guru one-pointedly, then real devotion will arise in us. Once we have this real devotion, we will be able to
receive the blessing of our root guru and all the lamas that have come before
us. If we look at it from the viewpoint of the sutra path, in guru yoga we will
be receiving all the blessings that have come from Buddha Shakyamuni, all
the way down to all the various teachers that came after Buddha Shakyamuni. If however, we consider guru yoga from the viewpoint of the
Vajrayana, we will see that we will be receiving the blessings of all the ones
that have come from Vajradhara or Dorje Chang, all the way down to us.[19]

Guru yoga practice is the process of merging the minds and the blessings
of the Buddhas and bodhisattvas with ours. It's like the merging of two rivers
into one. So through the practice of guru yoga, our shamatha meditation
and vipashyana meditation will arise quickly and our meditation will be very
clear due to the practice of guru yoga. Whether we are doing the creation
stage or the completion stage of deity meditation all of it will become much
clearer and comes much more quickly through this practice.

The Superior Preliminaries

The preliminaries to mahamudra include the usual preliminaries of the four
thoughts (the general preliminaries) and ngondro (the special preliminaries),

which I have now discussed and also some superior preliminaries, which are called the four conditions.

These four superior preliminaries are unique to mahamudra practice. They are unlike the ngondro, in that they are not practices that need to be done separately. They are four things you need to understand and keep in mind about the environment or circumstances surrounding the practice of meditation. If you understand these four things, which are called the four conditions for practice, then you will greatly enhance your practice of both the shamatha and the vipashyana aspects of mahamudra.

The Causal Condition: Revulsion of Samsara

The first of the four conditions is revulsion. Revulsion here is called the causal condition, because it is the fundamental condition that must be present for meditation to occur. Essentially, revulsion here means that recollection of the fact that, having been born as human beings, we must make some appropriate use of this opportunity that we possess.[20] Ideally of course, we would like to completely relinquish with our mind the things of this life and this world. But that may be an unrealistic ambition. We can, however, at least lessen our fixation on and our obsession with the things of this life by recognizing that, while indeed we have mundane responsibilities that we need to fulfil, nevertheless, the practice of dharma is of the greatest importance. Through recognizing the importance of the practice of dharma and the relative unimportance of the things of this life, one begins to cultivate revulsion. In general, of course, one cultivates revulsion through the meditations on the four general preliminaries already discussed. Among these four, that which is especially important in this context is the recollection of impermanence. The recollection of impermanence, which encourages one to practice to begin with, and the resulting revulsion it generates, are the causal condition, the first of the four conditions.

If, from the beginning, you can recollect impermanence easily, of course this is excellent. But when people start to meditate upon impermanence, they often find that it saddens them so much that they regard it as an unpleasant thing to think about. Nevertheless, impermanence and even the sadness that it inspires are of great benefit. According to the Buddha, there are three principal benefits to meditation on impermanence. The initial benefit is that impermanence, or the recollection of impermanence, is the condition that inspires one to practice dharma in the first place. It is through some understanding of impermanence that one is initially inspired to begin to practice, to enter the door of dharma. You might ask, "Having entered the door of dharma, does one then abandon the recollection of impermanence?" One does not, because subsequently, impermanence is that which encourages diligence. If one does not continue to recollect impermanence, then in spite of one's initial inspiration, one might lose heart, or one might lose interest in dharma. For example, people often come to me and say, "I like dharma, but I cannot make myself practice. What can I do to remedy this?" I always reply, "Meditate on impermanence!"

And finally, impermanence is said to be the companion that leads to fruition, which means that the continued recollection of impermanence during the path is what actually causes one to continue along the path and causes one to attain the result. At best, of course, the result is the supreme siddhi, but at least, through practice, one will generate a state of contentment with the way one has lived one's life through having used it in the practice of dharma. In these ways, the recollection of impermanence is absolutely essential and is therefore called the causal condition for the practice of meditation. Therefore, continue to think about impermanence. Do not neglect the contemplation of impermanence, thinking that, because it is so depressing to think about, it is best to avoid it.

The Principal Condition: Reliance Upon the Guru

The second of the four conditions is called the principal condition. The principal condition refers to reliance upon the guru. The guru here refers to four different aspects of the guru.

a) A Guru of the Lineage

The first is the guru of the lineage, who is an individual or a person. The reason one needs to rely upon another person who can function as a teacher or guru, and who holds an authentic lineage, is that, whereas in the case of mundane activities there are no doubt some things that one can figure out on one's own, in the case of the samadhis of shamatha and vipashyana, which are beyond the conventions of this world, one definitely needs the authoritative instruction of an individual with experience of these things. Therefore, one needs to rely upon a personal teacher or root guru. This root guru must hold an unbroken lineage of practical experience passed from one experienced individual to another. In short, the basic instructions of meditation cannot be gained simply through reading books, or [by figuring it out by oneself, or from unqualified teachers without authentic lineage.]

books
b) The Dictates of the Sugatas

However, while relying upon the root guru, the personal guru who holds the lineage, one comes also to rely upon the second guru, which is the dictates of the Sugatas, or the teachings of the Buddha [and other realized beings]. While one bases one's practice upon the oral instructions of one's root guru, one augments this by studying the teachings of the Buddha, the commentaries on his teachings by the great mahasiddhas, and the texts of instruction of the lineage of practice and accomplishment. Through augmenting the oral instructions of one's guru in this way, one clarifies and reinforces them by relying upon the written teachings of other Buddhas and bodhisattvas. It is therefore important to actively pursue the study of dharma texts. In this connection, people often ask, "Which of the many books that there are should we read?" You should principally study texts that talk about the practice of meditation, especially those that come from a lineage of experiential instruction and unbroken transmission of experience. Through doing this you will both clarify the instructions that you have previously received, so that things that you may not have understood will become clear to you, and also you will remind yourself of aspects of the teachings or instructions that you may have forgotten. Therefore, the second type of guru is the dictates of the sugatas.

With regard to this type of study, which is reliance upon the second aspect of the guru, if one studies out of mere curiosity, the desire to know more and more about dharma, then this is, in general, okay, but it is not really the appropriate approach to study for a meditator. In general, the way in which a practitioner should study is to search for instructions that will remedy specific problems one is experiencing with meditation. If one's meditation is afflicted by lack of clarity, one should look for and study that which will enhance the clarity of one's meditation. If one's meditation is afflicted by lack of stability, one should look for and study that which will enhance the stability of one's meditation. If one feels that one lacks faith and devotion, one should look for and study methods that will help to generate further faith and devotion. If one feels that one lacks adequate revulsion, one should look for and study that which will generate further revulsion. You study in order to improve your practice, not in order to acquire knowledge that you can then repeat to others, or use as a basis for debate with others. In short, if you study in order to learn more about how to practice properly, then there will be great benefit in it. That is the proper reliance upon the second aspect of the guru, which is the dictates of the sugatas.

c) The Guru of Dharmata

The third aspect of the guru is the guru of dharmata or absolute truth. This is what one comes to realize through relying upon the first two aspects of the guru. Through the oral instructions of one's personal guru and the information one acquires from the guru, which are the teachings of Buddhas and bodhisattvas, one comes to be able to realize the nature of things or dharmata. This nature of things, which can be realized and which is to be realized, is this third aspect of the guru. In general, it can be called dharmata, the nature of all things, or in the specific context of mahamudra, the nature of the mind itself. In any case, this which is to be realized is the third aspect of the guru, the absolute guru of dharmata.

d) The Sign Guru of Appearances

The fourth guru is the sign guru of appearances or experiences, which is the arising of what appears to you as signs or indications of dharma. By appearances or experiences we mean, first of all, those things which appear to us as external objects—visible forms, sounds, smells, tastes and tactile sensations—all of which are, in absolute truth, emptiness, but which nevertheless appear unimpededly as relative truths. By appearances and experiences we also mean the thoughts that arise in your mind: thoughts of pleasure and displeasure, of suffering and joy, and so on. This unimpeded variety of internal thoughts and external appearances is what is referred to as appearances or experience. Appearances in themselves, because they demonstrate the nature of things, are always a sign or an indication of that nature, and are therefore called the sign guru of appearances. Of course, if you fixate on appearances, then these appearances become a condition that casts you further into samsara. But if you look at them in a different way, without fixation, then appearances themselves become the guru, because the impermanence of appearances is a reminder of impermanence. And the emptiness of appearances is an indication of emptiness. Appearances and their change and their variety can inspire devotion and so on. It is not the case that appearances in and of themselves teach you dharma per se; they rather demonstrate it, or embody it. Therefore, if you understand appearances, if you recognize them to be as they are, then they are always signs of dharma, signs of the illusory nature of appearances, signs of the dreamlike nature of things, and so on. Therefore, the recognition of appearances is the fourth guru, the sign guru of appearances.

The reliance upon these four aspects of the guru is the second condition, the principal condition.

The Focal Condition: Direct Recognition of the Mind's Nature

The third condition is called the focal condition and refers to that on which you are focusing, to that which you are attempting to realize through your practice of meditation. It refers to the object of the shamatha and vipashyana meditations of mahamudra. Here, however, the object of meditation is not something that is produced through speculative analysis, or [through] any other kind of philosophical system, and it is completely divorced from any kind of adherence to any kind of intellectual stance or position. Here the object of meditation is the direct recognition of the nature of things, just as they are, which is therefore far superior to and very different in characteristics from the ascertainment of things through analysis. That nature of things is the focal condition, or the object of the mahamudra meditations of shamatha and vipashyana.

With regard to this focal condition, the nature of things is presented differently in the various vehicles or aspects of dharma. For example, in the common vehicle[21] it is basically presented as selflessness, in particular the selflessness of persons, the lack of inherent existence of persons. The benefit of this presentation is obvious. Since the root of all kleshas is fixation on a personal self, then the discovery, through rigorous analysis, that there is no personal self produces some liberation from this fixation, because one has recognized that this fixation is based upon a fundamental mistake and is therefore unnecessary. For that reason then, the selflessness of persons is presented. In other contexts and other vehicles it is presented that the nature of things is the emptiness of all things without exception, and through coming to understand that emptiness, one comes to gradually free oneself from fixation, not only on this falsely imputed personal self, but also on falsely imputed external things as well. Here, however, in this uncommon or special tradition of practical instruction, we concern ourselves only with the nature of the mind. We do so, first, because the root of all of our pleasure and pain is not external things in and of themselves, but the mind that generates these attitudes or experiences. Therefore, resolution—coming to a definitive understanding—of the nature of one's mind is of foremost importance. We concern ourselves only with the nature of mind, secondly, because the nature of the mind is very easy to view and can be viewed directly by anyone. It does not need to be speculated upon or figured out through analysis. There is no need to generate expectations about what the nature of the mind is, based upon an adherence to a specific tradition, and there is no need to fabricate some kind of understanding of the mind's nature through analysis. The nature of mind can be directly recognized. Therefore, the focal condition in this context of mahamudra is the direct recognition of the mind's nature, just as it is, without any kind of adherence to any intellectually contrived view.

The focal condition is essentially the object or concern or focus of the meditation itself, which one focuses on through the methods of both shamatha and vipashyana. Initially, one uses the shamatha technique to calm the mind to the point where its nature can be easily viewed or discerned. Then one uses the two aspects of vipashyana—viewing [or looking at] the mind, and identifying or pointing out the mind's nature—in order to gradually come to a decisive recognition of that nature.

The Immediate Condition: The Absence of Hope or Anxiety About One's Progress in Meditation

The fourth condition is called the immediate or direct condition. This is the direct circumstance that is the immediate or direct cause of, or condition for, meditation. This is the absence of fixation on meditation and the contents of meditation experience, which means being without great hope for or anxiety about progress in one's meditation, the clarity of one's meditative state, and so on. It is to apply oneself in a stable way with continuous exertion to the practice of meditation without any specific hope for acquiring a certain result. It is being without the thought, "I am meditating. This meditative state is unclear. I must make it clear. Oh, this is not empty. I must somehow cause it to appear to be empty, because I expect it to be empty," and so on. Being without such fabrication, such kinds of hope and anxiety, is this fourth condition.

The attitude that one's meditation must become good and that one must have pleasant experiences will tend to corrupt one's practice of meditation. You need to take the attitude that, if meditation experiences of whatever kind occur, that is fine; if they do not, that is also fine. If you do not take that kind of uncompromising attitude towards experiences that arise, then whenever a particularly pleasant or particularly lucid experience of meditation occurs, you will make a big deal out of it. In fact, you will, in your memory of it, exaggerate it. Therefore, fixating on this exaggerated memory of that pleasant or lucid meditation experience, naturally, in your next session, you will be disappointed, because what you are fixating on is, in fact, an exaggeration of what occurred. That disappointment will have repercussions that will gradually corrupt your practice. Therefore, in your practice you simply need to rest in the nature of whatever arises; whether your meditation experience is pleasant or unpleasant, is lucid or torpid—it makes no difference. In any case, simply observe the nature of whatever arises. That is the fourth condition, the immediate or direct condition.

These four conditions are not separate meditation practices. It is not the case that you begin a session thinking, "I am now going to meditate on the focal condition;" or "I am now going to meditate on the principal condition," and so on. These are things about the basic environment or circumstances of meditation practice in general, however, that need to be understood and kept in mind. Through an understanding and recollection of these four conditions, then if you lack exertion, you will develop exertion; if your meditation lacks lucidity, it will develop lucidity. These four conditions are equally important for somebody beginning the practice of meditation and for someone who is already experienced with the practice of meditation. All practitioners really need to rely upon and recollect these four conditions. However, while these four conditions need to be kept in mind, they are not separate practices that are cultivated separately from the main practice.

3 SHAMATHA (TRANQUILITY) MEDITATION

THE STAGES OF MAHAMUDRA practice consist of the preliminaries, which has now been covered, the main practice, and the conclusion. The main practice of mahamudra is divided into two aspects: tranquility (shamatha) meditation, and insight (vipashyana) meditation.

Of these two aspects of meditation, it is vipashyana that leads to the ultimate result or fruition. But for vipashyana to be both stable and lucid it must be thoroughly grounded in shamatha. The reason for this is that our minds are actually very agitated and move about a great deal. So for vipashyana to be stable, it is necessary that we initially calm our mind through the practice of shamatha. If you have received the pointing out of vipashyana, then the subsequent practice of shamatha will only increase and stabilize the lucidity of your recognition. If you have not yet received that pointing out, then the practice of shamatha is essential in order to enable you to receive it in the future.

Now, shamatha meditation is absolutely necessary, not only in the ultimate sense, but also in the short term by bringing great benefit when we practice it. When we have not practiced meditation, our thought processes are entirely beyond our control, and we are victimized by the arising of all manner of thoughts. We have both virtuous and negative thoughts: virtuous thoughts are thoughts of love and compassion and altruism, while negative thoughts are thoughts of attachment, anger, ignorance, and so on. Proportionately the greater number of thoughts are negative ones, which create problems.

We can look at our thoughts in another way. Some of our thoughts are pleasant—in other words, thoughts that make us happy or make us feel good—and some are unpleasant, thoughts that make us unhappy, that make us worry unnecessarily, that make us mentally and, finally, physically agitated. But if we compare these two, we'll see that, proportionately, the thoughts that actually make us happy arise comparatively rarely, while the thoughts that make us worried and agitated seem to arise constantly. When we are under the sway of negative thoughts, initially we are unhappy and eventually we become unhealthy. If we can arrest this process and gain control over it, then initially we'll become happy, and this in turn will keep us from becoming physically agitated and unhealthy as well.

If there were a practical need to follow after or entertain these agitating thoughts, if they actually helped us to function better, that would be one thing, but in fact they do not. The disturbing emotions we generate, such as attachment and aversion, and the agitation they bring up are unnecessary and do not make us function more effectively at all. Since they do not improve our functioning and since they make us unhappy, they are, from any point of view, unnecessary and of no benefit. In the short term, in the present time of practice, there is an obvious and great benefit if you can arrest this process of being victimized by uncontrolled thoughts and allow your mind to rest naturally and evenly. In the long term, you can achieve real freedom. The basic quality of this process of victimization by thought is that thoughts seem to be beyond our control. We have no freedom of mind. It's as though we're wafted about on the surface of a body of water by fierce waves. In this analogy the waves are our thoughts. When we start to practice meditation, thoughts are not arrested immediately because we have a very strong and deeply entrenched habit of being controlled by our thoughts. But as we practice, gradually we gain freedom from the influence of thoughts. And this freedom consists of the emergence of space in our experience, a spaciousness that allows our innate wisdom to manifest over and beyond the controlling thoughts. That is the ultimate benefit of shamatha meditation.

Points of the Body (Posture in Meditation)

The actual practice of shamatha meditation involves two techniques: the physical posture and the meditation performed by the mind. Of course, the actual meditator is your mind, not your body. Nevertheless, because our mind and body are so intimately connected, if we take a correct physical posture, it makes it much easier for the mind to meditate properly. There are two general ways that the correct physical posture is taught. One is the five-fold meditation posture,[22] which is explained elsewhere. In this particular text and tradition, the sevenfold posture called the seven dharmas of Vairochana is taught. This technique is named after the Buddha Vairochana, whose name has dual significance. First, the literal meaning of Vairochana is "the utterly radiant," giving the idea that the posture allows our mind to rest naturally so that the inherent clarity of the mind is enhanced. Second, the Buddha Vairochana is the pure nature of the aggregate of form, which includes our physical body. So the idea is that we're making the most appropriate and best possible use of our form aggregate through physical posture to enhance meditation.

This posture has seven aspects, the first being the placement of the legs, which should be crossed. Typically most texts say that they should be in the position called vajra asana, or full lotus, which means with the legs fully crossed and the feet resting on the opposite thighs. The reason this particular form of cross-legged posture is extolled is that it creates a great deal of physical stability. However, it's fine if you take another cross-legged posture, it needn't be that one in particular. The significance of sitting cross-legged is to allow your mind to come to rest in a way that is neither too dull nor too agitated. If you attempt to meditate while standing, you'll find that your mind is somewhat agitated or excited. If, on the other hand, you attempt to meditate while lying down, you'll find that your mind will tend to be a little too dull. Sitting cross-legged is the compromise between these two. If you cannot sit cross-legged for a physical reason, it is also perfectly acceptable to sit in a chair.

The second point of posture is the placement of the hands. It's said the hands should be even. This is interpreted in two ways, both of which are acceptable. One refers to the mudra, or gesture, of even placement, which is the position of the hands in the manner of the Buddha Amitabha. In this case, the left hand is placed palm up in your lap close to your body, and the right hand is placed in or on the left hand. The actual significance of the term "even placement of the hands" is that the hands be placed at the same level. Because if one of your hands, for example, is held aloft in space and the other one is put on the ground, the difference in level or placement of the hands will induce an instability or excitement of mind. By keeping your hands at the same level, your mind naturally settles down. Therefore, it's also acceptable to place your hands palms down on the thighs, that is to say, your right hand on the right thigh and your left hand on the left thigh, slightly behind the knees, in the position often seen in pictures of Marpa.

The third point is that the body is straight, which means that the upper body and especially the spine should be as straight as possible. The main point here is not to be lazy and slouch. Texts on meditation commonly state that if the body is straight, the subtle channels within the body will be straight, and if the channels within the body are straight, then the winds will flow freely. And if the winds flow freely, the mind will settle naturally.[23] Now, if you sit with your body leaning to the left or to the right or leaning forward or backward or hunched over, then your mind naturally is not in a state of rest. If you sit up straight, the channels straighten and the winds move freely, and as a result, your mind will settle because the relationship between the mind and the winds—or the fundamental energies within your body—is like the relationship between a rider and the horse on which the rider rides. If the winds are flowing naturally and freely through the straightening of the channels, then the mind will naturally come to rest. On the other hand, if the channels are all twisted or bent, then your mind will be unstable as well.

The fourth point is the position of the arms, which is that the arms should be like the spread wings of a vulture. What this means simply is that the elbows are not held against the body. The reason for this is that exerting enough effort in the posture so that the elbows are spread a bit outward from the body promotes a further clarity in your mind. If you're taking the posture with the right hand placed in the left hand in your lap, then instead of bringing your elbows against your body, you put the elbows slightly outward like spread wings. And if you're taking the posture with the hands palms down on the thighs, then rather than allowing your elbows to sink, you bring them up somewhat, straighten the arms a little bit, in order to induce more clarity in your mind.

The fifth point is that the neck should be slightly bent or hooked. If you allow the position of your neck to remain as it often is in daily life with your chin stuck out and looking slightly upward, then you'll become distracted, because this posture is induced by and also brings about a state of mental distraction. The reason why this posture generates distraction is that it's one in which your mindfulness and alertness are naturally at an ebb, or reduced level. In fact, by slightly bringing the chin back in, which is what's meant by bending the neck, you promote mindfulness and alertness, and you will be less likely to become distracted.[24]

The sixth point is that the tongue should touch the palate. The reason for this is simply that when you relax your body and your mind in meditation, you will tend to produce a lot of saliva. If you constantly need to be swallowing saliva, this will begin to disturb you. To be less disturbed by this, you touch your tongue to the palate.

The seventh point is the gaze. The gaze is very important in meditation, because we are so visual that our thoughts generally follow our vision. The first point with regard to gaze is that the eyes should neither be gaping wide open nor be clamped shut. If your eyelids are gaping wide so that you're glaring, this tends to cause your mind to become involved with the visual consciousness. If, on the other hand, you close your eyes, this tends to cause a certain mental dullness. In order that neither of these defects occur, allow your eyes to remain naturally open, without directing your attention to what you see and without thinking about what you see. Of course, you will continue to see, but simply don't consciously direct your attention to it. In that way, your vision becomes slightly relaxed. Now, with regard to the actual direction of the gaze, it is said to be four finger widths in front of the tip of your nose in space, which means that you're looking slightly downward, not straight downward—but slightly downward. This often confuses people, because normally when you look at something you don't look at the midst of nothing or in the midst of space. It's not a problem if your eyes are naturally some distance away, but don't intentionally focus on anything; just let your vision naturally relax. Don't try to focus on anything, and don't try not to focus on anything.

These are the seven points of posture called the seven dharmas of Vairochana. After presenting these points in the text, a further instruction is given. This is, don't be too tight in holding the posture, which means don't exert physical tension in order to maintain it. In other words, relax. Let the posture be natural and comfortable. When some people practice meditation, they are too tense in their posture and become physically exhausted. Or, if they are too tense with their gaze, they'll find that they produce a lot of tears. To eliminate these problems simply relax the muscles in your body and do not attempt to hold them with any kind of tension. The most important lineage guru in the lineage of Chod, or "cutting through," was the famous woman siddha Machig Labchi Dronma, who said, "The essence of physical posture is to relax the four limbs," which means to relax the muscles in the arms and legs. While you need to maintain the Vairochana physical posture, at the same time, you need to do it in a way that is relaxed and natural.

When some people meditate, they generate a great deal of tension, which produces discomfort and pain. Usually this type of physical tension comes from having a mind that's too tight. When you're practicing meditation, you're training in mindfulness and alertness and need to check from time to time to make sure that you're not producing physical tension in your body.

After having adopted the physical posture, you should next expel the dead air. "Dead air" means the air you've breathed in and used up and are ready to breathe out. Expelling it doesn't mean anything dramatic; it simply means making sure that you breathe out fully. This is done three times, consciously and intentionally but without much effort, thinking with each breath that you are expelling all sickness, all demonic disturbances, and all disturbing emotions. This is done only at the beginning of a meditation session. After expelling this stale or dead air three times, allow yourself to breathe completely naturally. Just as you relax the physical posture and attempt to be natural with that, so too should you allow the breathing to be natural.

Points of the Mind (Mental Technique)

The second aspect of the shamatha meditation is the mental technique, which has two aspects: the basic technique and the particular techniques.

(a) General Points of the Mind

The general or basic technique is as follows. First of all, our mind is utterly insubstantial and yet, at the same time, has the ability to know, to experience, and so on. Fundamentally, shamatha meditation consists of allowing this mind that is insubstantial and yet can know or experience to relax naturally. Most of the thoughts that run through our minds are concerned with either the past or the future. We often think of the past; thinking, "I met so and so, I said such and such, I did this and that; last year I did this, last month I did that." In short, a lot of our thoughts are memories. We think a lot, as well, about the future. We plan and fantasize and think, "Next year I will do this, next month I will do that, for the rest of my life I will do such and such." Of course, we need to plan for the future, but we do not need to do so constantly. So the first part of the technique is to simply not prolong the past nor beckon the future. In other words, don't think about the past and don't think about the future. Instead, simply relax in a direct experience of the present moment.

With regard to this awareness of the present moment, our mind is utterly insubstantial and yet has this characteristic of luminosity (Tib. *salwa*). "Luminosity" here simply means the cognitive capacity, the fact that our mind can know, experience, feel, and so on. This awareness always occurs in the present. When we are not thinking of the past or thinking of the future, when we're letting our mind simply rest in the direct experience of the present moment, then this awareness or lucidity emerges as an unfabricated intelligence. Initially we do this very briefly, for one moment, two moments, and so on, but as we work with this, it starts to take on a momentum. However, it's important not to interfere with the naturalness of this awareness by appraising what is occurring, which means that we shouldn't think, "Well, this is happening, that is happening, I'm aware of this, I'm aware of that." Nor should we judge what's happening by thinking, "Well, this is good, this is what's supposed to be happening," or, "This is bad, this isn't what's supposed to be happening." On the other hand, we do need to "plant the watchman of mindfulness and alertness," which means that we maintain some intentional awareness of what is occurring. Here, mindfulness means a simple, direct recollection of what we're trying to do. In other words, mindfulness is recollecting that we are trying to rest in a direct experience of the present moment. Alertness then is that faculty of mind that becomes aware when we become distracted from this present experience. However, this watchfulness or, this watchman, has to be very relaxed and gentle. It can't be too heavy-handed, otherwise the whole thing becomes a conceptual judgement. The technique of mind is to rest in this awareness of the present moment with a gentle watchman of mindfulness and alertness.

(b) Particular Points of the Mind

In addition to the basic technique, there are a number of particular techniques, involving a variety of supports that are appropriate to use when we find that our mind simply cannot come to rest. Most teachers have emphasized using the breath. This is a very good way to practice shamatha, because, as was said by the Buddha, "If you are afflicted by a great many thoughts, or a great deal of conceptuality, then follow the breath." Therefore, most teachers of the Theravada, Mahayana and Vajrayana traditions emphasize following the breath as the fundamental technique of shamatha meditation. However, in the specific context of mahamudra as presented in this specific text, *Pointing Out the Dharmakaya,* a number of different shamatha methods are given, and I will attempt to go through these briefly.

The first group of techniques uses the sense consciousnesses as a basis for establishing shamatha. One can use the eye consciousness, the ear consciousness, or the tactile consciousness, and so on. First presented is how to use the eye consciousness. The eye consciousness, of course, is the medium though which we see form. Usually when we observe form, we generate a thought or concept on the basis of what we observe, and we become distracted. Here the technique or discipline, is to allow one's gaze to rest on one specific form and then rest in that without becoming distracted.

There are a variety of ways one could use the eyes as the basis for shamatha meditation. Because some of them might produce more enthusiasm in the practitioner and therefore more benefit than others, six techniques are presented. The first of these uses a pebble as a support for the practice. One places a pebble on a surface in front of one and simply looks at it, or gazes at it. This does not involve analysis of the pebble's characteristics; one does not think about the shape, size, or color of the pebble. One simply allows one's gaze to rest on the pebble, and one remains in that state in which one is physically seeing the pebble and does not lose track of the presence of it. But one does not engage in conceptualization about it.

The second technique uses a statue or image of the Buddha as a support for the practice. This is called a pure or sacred support. In general, we use statues of the Buddha in order to inculcate faith and devotion, and here that is fine. But faith and devotion are not the most essential point of the practice. One simply uses the image of the Buddha as a support for one's bare attention, as one did with the pebble. The superiority of this technique lies in the fact that the blessing of the Buddha's form somehow empowers or enhances the shamatha that is developed. As in the previous technique one simply places the image in the line of one's gaze and observes it without losing track of its presence, but without analyzing it. While one is practicing, if one's mind becomes torpid or agitated, there are remedies in connection with this technique that may be applied. If our mind becomes torpid then we should raise our gaze so that, rather than looking at the center of the body of the image, we are looking at the head, and in particular, at the ushnishna, or crown protuberance. If, on the other hand, our mind becomes agitated or excited, then we should lower our gaze to the feet or the lotus and moon seat on which the Buddha is sitting. If our mind is neither agitated nor torpid, and has a natural clarity that is not conceptual, then we can either direct our attention all at once to the whole form of the image, or to the heart in particular.

When you have gained the ability to rest your mind on the image of the Buddha, then you move on to the third technique. The difference between the first two and the third technique is that, whereas the first two supports — the mundane support of the pebble and the sacred support of the image of the Buddha — were both very solid, hard objects, now, in the third technique — in order to gradually refine the attention based on refining the object — we use the flame of a lamp, such as a butter lamp. Of course, a flame is still form, but it is less solid, and therefore is getting closer, in a sense, to resting our mind in emptiness. In other respects however, the quality of the attention we bring to gazing at the flame is the same as in the first two techniques.

The fourth technique, which is taken up when the third is mastered, is even more subtle, because here we look at a space. The particular type of space that we look at is a hole or an aperture, as the hole in a wall, or in a piece of paper, or something like that. The hole should not be larger than the palm of your hand and can be any convenient amount smaller than that. In any case, we direct our attention to the place in the aperture, and not to the material surrounding it.

Once you have practiced the fourth technique, then you move on to the fifth, which uses the three syllables, OM AH HUNG, which represent or embody, the body, speech, and mind respectively of all the Buddhas and bodhisattvas. You begin by actually having in front of you a written or drawn white syllable OM, which represents the body of all Buddhas and bodhisattvas; a red AH, which represents their speech; and a blue HUNG which represents their mind. Once you have gained ability in resting your mind on this actually present image, then you dispense with the physical support and visualize the three syllables, resting your mind on that visualization.

Once you have mastered that, then you move on to the sixth technique in which, instead of visualizing the three syllables, you simply visualize three spheres of light of those corresponding colors: a white sphere of light, which represents the body of all the Buddhas and bodhisattvas; a red sphere, which represents their speech; and a blue sphere, which represents their mind.[25]

Again, you can begin by drawing a depiction of this and once your mind is able to rest on that, then you can simply visualize them. All of these six techniques are basically working with visually perceived form, and therefore, with the eye consciousness.

In all six techniques, you maintain a bare attention directed at the object so that you remain with a bare awareness of it, from which you never depart. As for the use of these six techniques, while there is a gradual refinement observable in their sequence, it is not necessarily the case that any one practitioner needs to practice all six. You can use any of these techniques, or any number among them, as you see fit. In any case, when using such a support, whichever one it is, you should not conceptualize or evaluate the support. You should not speculate upon its substantiality or insubstantiality, and so on. As beginners, of course, we are still prey to hope and anxiety with regard to the results and quality of meditation. So, you should not allow yourself to get involved in the thought, "I need good meditation, I must have good meditation," or the thought, "I am afraid that such and such defects may arise in my meditation." Simply relax in an undistracted, bare mindfulness that is conjoined with alertness, based upon the use of the particular support, whichever one it is.

Although in these six techniques you are using the visual consciousness and, therefore, the eyes, you should not attempt to focus your eyes too harshly or too tightly upon the support. If you do, you may start to have visual hallucinations, such as the visual support's seeming to shake, and your eyes may come to hurt. If these things start to happen, then you should stop and learn to use the eyes in a much more relaxed way. In fact, not only the eyes but also the mind should be allowed to come to rest on the object in a very relaxed way.

The most common defect that arises when using this type of technique is torpor or mental obscurity. One should not allow these defects to continue uncorrected. As soon as you recognize the presence of torpor or mental obscurity, you should make efforts to introduce more clarity into the meditative state. That concludes the presentation of the first technique, which uses the eye consciousness.

Following this presentation are four similar techniques which make use of the other four sense consciousnesses. You can use the ear consciousness, the smell consciousness, the taste or tongue consciousness, and the tactile or physical consciousness. For example, using the ear consciousness, you simply direct your attention, not to what you see, but to what you hear. You may or may not be hearing something in particular, but by directing your attention to what you hear, you become aware of sound in general, and you rest your mind on that. In the same way, you can use the nose or olfactory consciousness, and simply direct your attention to what you are smelling. You may be smelling something pleasant or unpleasant, or a mixture of the two, or you may not be aware of smelling anything in particular. But in the same way, by directing your attention to this you become aware of smelling in general. Then you can direct your attention to the tongue and in the same way become aware of tastes, and to the body in general, and in that way become aware of tactile sensations. In all of these four techniques you rest your mind on these particular sensations just as you did with the visual forms in the first technique.

It often happens when you rest your mind using a specific technique of shamatha, that a thought arises and pulls your attention away from the technique, or distracts you from it. When thoughts arise, then do not get involved with the content of the thought. Simply recognize the arising of a thought in your mind, and pay very little attention to the contents of that thought. All you need to recognize is that the thought has arisen. Whether you consider it a bad thought or a good thought is irrelevant in this context. If a thought arises that is shockingly bad, don't entertain any guilt about it, and if it's a magnificent, virtuous, heroic thought, don't become excited about it. Sometimes thoughts present themselves as special; for example, you might think of something that you believe you really need to think about, such as what you're going to do about such and such later in the day. This can be very seductive. The way to deal with these attractive thoughts is to say to yourself, "Okay, I'll think about that later because right now I'm meditating." Then simply return to the technique, having acknowledged the importance of the thought and given it an appointment for later on.

Post-Meditation

What we have just discussed concerns the actual meditation practice of shamatha. Next comes the presentation of post-meditation practice. The principal problem that is addressed in the discussion of post-meditation is that we might tend to regard a meditation as a time of hard work and post-meditation as a time of relaxation or vacation. The problem with that attitude is that we then try to relax so much in the post-meditation that our minds become sloppy and, therefore, we lose the benefit of the meditation session. The remedy for this is to maintain an undistracted mindfulness that is appropriate to post-meditation activities, that is therefore distinct from the mindfulness of the meditation session, but that is nevertheless maintained and therefore brings post-meditation into the practice of meditation. Specifically, when one is practicing shamatha, one has to be careful in one's conduct of body, speech, and mind in order not to become so agitated that one loses the shamatha meditative state.

For example, with your body you should be careful with the use of your eyes and not gaze off in a distracted way into the distance, but look precisely, look close to yourself, even look at the point of the nose if necessary, and in that way remain mindful. Move slowly and decisively, be careful in all your movements. And also with your speech, be careful about what you say and do not rush into speaking carelessly, or speaking too fast and endlessly. And also with your mind, in post-meditation you need to be careful with the thoughts that arise. You should not allow coarse thoughts to take control of the mind, so therefore, you should not give in to coarse and wild thoughts, but try to maintain a relaxed state of mind in which, at least to some extent, the process of thinking is slowed down, or cooled down.

Remedies for Torpor & Excitement

All of these techniques, called the external placement of the mind, use some external support or perception as a basis for the mind's coming to rest. Presented next is the internal placement of the mind, which is principally concerned with specific remedies for the two defects of torpor and excitement. First of all, the basis for any remedy for torpor and excitement to be applied is the maintenance of a degree of mindfulness and alertness that will enable you to detect the presence of either of these defects. A shamatha practitioner needs constantly to maintain a kind of tough clarity of mindfulness and alertness, so that no matter what arises in the mind, it will be recognized. Then on the basis of that, one can apply the remedies.

When we are meditating, we need to relax into a state of stillness, which is to say where our mind is at rest, without impeding the mind's luminosity or lucidity. While we're practicing, there will arise a variety of experiences. Some of them are lucid, some of them are not lucid. Among the experiences which will arise, there are some that indicate defects in the meditation. Torpor has two varieties. There's what we could call torpor itself, and there's obscurity, which is a further development of that. Torpor is the absence of clarity, the absence of any cognitive lucidity in the meditation, and obscurity is even beyond that, where there's a thick dullness. Now the problem with torpor and obscurity is that obviously they bring about the disappearance of mindfulness and therefore of alertness as well. Excitement is when the lucidity of the mind becomes too intense and becomes conceptual and therefore the mind generates lots of thoughts — past, present, future and so on — that are so many and so intense that we can't stop them or let go of them. Now this can be either a pleasant or an unpleasant excitement. It could be excessive excitement in being too happy or too enthusiastic. Or it can be agitation, which is a thought that is basically unpleasant and disturbing. So excitement really consists of those two varieties, but in either case, excitement is the presence of thoughts that are of sufficient coarseness or force to disturb or unseat our meditation and thereby distract us from the technique.

Now, there are obviously a lot of things that can go wrong with meditation, but basically all of them are included within the two types of defects; torpor and excitement. The internal placement of the mind consists of using the appropriate remedies for these two defects.

There are three things we can do in general to get rid of either of these defects. The three things are what we could call; external changes, visualization and using motivation.

If we look at torpor, first of all, using motivation to get rid of torpor can be effective, because the nature of torpor is a mental dullness, which is to some extent, a lack of motivation. So therefore, recollecting the qualities of the dharma and of the Buddha and recollecting the benefits of meditation can sometimes promote the clarity that will cut through the torpor.

A second method for working with dullness or torpor is by physical means, by turning up the lights and making sure the body is not too warm by opening up a window or taking off any warm clothes. Third when we are experiencing torpor, we can visualize in our heart, which is to say in our body at the level of the heart, a white four-petalled lotus, which is very, very bright and brilliant, and in the centre of this lotus a tiny white sphere of light. Then having visualized that, we think that the sphere of light comes up through the centre of our body and shoots out the top of our head. That visualization is very helpful for dispelling torpor.

There are three corresponding ways to work with excitement.

Generally speaking, excitement can come from either pleasant or unpleasant mental states. We could be excited or agitated by guilt, for example, or we could be agitated or excited by something that makes us very happy, that we can't stop thinking about. In either case, the basic problem is that the thoughts keep coming back again and again and again, and we can't get rid of them. Generally speaking, the way to work with motivation here is to cultivate some sadness. Sadness is very helpful for dealing with excitement, so we could contemplate the defects of samsara, the sufferings of the lower realms, impermanence and so on. Generally speaking, anything that lessens clinging, fixation and attachment will help with the problem of excitement.

The second way to work with excitement is making external changes in the environment. With torpor we wanted everything bright and cool, and our physical posture as erect as possible. Here we can actually slump a little bit, and it may help calm us down. The room in which we meditate should be not too bright if we're suffering from excitement, and we should make sure it is warm enough. Third, in the case of excitement in our meditation we visualize a jet black four-petalled lotus in our heart, with a little sphere of light in its centre which is also black. This time, instead of going up, we think that this little sphere of light drops down from the lotus, going straight down the middle of our body, out of the bottom, and keeps on going down into the ground. This will help to calm you down.

Placing the Mind Without Support

A further aspect of meditation, beyond the external and internal placement of the mind, is called placement of the mind without support whatsoever. This refers to using the elements and the dissolution of the elements, one into another, as a basis for the mind's coming to rest. This technique involves visualizing the elements in their essential form. So, earth is visualized as a square — not an entirely flat square, but not really a cube either, a square with some thickness — of yellow light. Then, behind that we visualize water in the form of a disk, again with some thickness, of white light. Behind that, fire in the form of a triangle of red light, pointing downwards. Behind that, wind or air, in the form of a semi-circle of green light [with the flat side up], and behind that, space, as a tetrahedron of blue light. This is like an upside down three-sided pyramid. Following that, we then visualize that they dissolve one into another. Having clearly visualized this, we think that then the earth dissolves into the water, the water dissolves into the fire, the fire dissolves into the air, the air dissolves into the space, and the space subsides into emptiness.

When you use this technique, then eventually your mind will come to rest in a state without thought, and then you maintain that state, using an appropriate degree of force to your mindfulness and alertness. Sometimes your mindfulness will need to be quite relaxed and at other times exerted. When it is relaxed, the mindfulness needs to be just enough bare attention so that you do not become distracted, so that you do not forget. When your mind is afflicted by either the tendency toward torpor or the tendency toward excitement, then you need to increase the exertion or power of your mindfulness. You need to exert the amount of force or energy of mindfulness necessary to keep yourself from becoming distracted by either torpor or excitement. It is taught that, in fact, no thought will arise in your mind at this point until you become distracted. So, when a thought arises, that is the beginning of distraction. However, if when a thought arises, you do not become involved in the content of the thought—which means neither following the thought, nor examining the thought, nor evaluating whether it is a good or bad thought, and so on—but merely recognize the arising of the thought, then the thought itself becomes the next object of your attention in this technique. In that way, you practice the technique that is called resting the mind on emptiness.

Resting the Mind on the Breath

The next technique of shamatha given here is resting the mind on the breath. This is different from the common technique of resting the mind on the breath, because here it uses the specific approach to breathing that is called *vase breathing*. Here, however, vase breathing is somewhat different from the way it is practiced when you are doing tummo[26] practice. Here it begins with the dispelling of the stale air, which is done in a nine-fold sequence. First of all, you block one of your nostrils with the hand on that side. So for example, you could block your left nostril with your left hand, or your right nostril with your right hand, it does not matter which. Then, through the other nostril that is left open, you exhale the stale air three times. The first time you exhale very, very gently; the second time somewhat more vigorously; and the third time quite forcefully. Then you repeat the same process of three-fold exhalation on the other side. So, if you began by blocking the left nostril when breathing out through the right, then, during the second set of breaths, you block the right nostril and again breathe out three times, first very gently, then more vigorously and finally forcefully through the left nostril. Having done six exhalations, you then place your hands on top of your knees and you breathe out this time through both nostrils, again gently the first time, vigorously the second, and forcefully the third.

The difference between this process of nine-fold exhalation and the way it is practiced as a preliminary for tummo is that in this case as you do it you simply block off the nostrils any way that is comfortable or convenient. Whereas if you are doing it as part of the tummo practice, then there are elaborate gestures, such as lotus wheels and so forth, which accompany all of this.

Following those nine exhalations, when you breathe in the next time, you do so particularly slowly and gently, and as you breathe the air in you think that you are bringing it in and down to below the navel. Then you actually press it down gently so that the air that you breathe is all contained as low down in your body as possible, thinking that it is below the navel, and you rest your mind on that part of the body below the navel where the wind is felt to be held. You conceive of this as an empty space that is now filled with this air or wind you have breathed in. You hold the breath for a short time and when it becomes uncomfortable, then you breathe out, and so forth. You should not attempt to hold the breath in this way when your stomach is particularly full, or particularly empty. This technique is especially advised for the early morning; it is supposed to be very beneficial. The most important thing about this technique is that the wind not be held or retained in the upper chest. When you have breathed in and are holding the breath by pushing it down into the lower part of your body, then it becomes a basis, not only for the mind naturally coming to rest, but also the holding of the breath will not cause any negative side effects physically.[27]

When we are practicing shamatha in these ways, for some people it happens relatively quickly that their mind comes to rest, for other people it takes a long time and seems to be very difficult. If the latter is the case, do not become discouraged at how long it takes to develop a state of stable shamatha. In most cases, the initial experience that we have of our mind starting to come to rest is called the "waterfall experience," where it actually seems to the practitioner that there are more thoughts than before. Our thoughts seem to flow through our mind with the speed and agitation of water flowing over a waterfall. In fact, there are not any more thoughts than there were before. What is happening is that for the first time we are starting to recognize how many thoughts are arising in our mind all the time. Previously when we had not practiced meditation, we were not aware of this, so there seemed in fact to be fewer thoughts running through our mind. Because this is the beginning of recognition and stability, it is considered to be a good experience and should not cause us to be discouraged, although it is, of course, the experience of a beginner.

If we continue, then gradually this waterfall-like experience will become an experience of the presence or movement of thoughts in our mind that is like a "slowly flowing river." Finally we will experience stable tranquility which is like a "still ocean without waves."[28]

Tightening, Loosening, and Turning Away

As we pass gradually through these various shamatha experiences, there are three techniques we need to integrate into our meditation: tension, relaxation, and reversal. The first, tension means to tighten both our body and our mind so that we produce a sensitivity in our attention or awareness that will prevent us from becoming distracted. This technique of tightening up our body and mind should be practiced for very short intervals.

The second technique, which is sometimes used in alternation with the first, is relaxation. In this technique we consciously relax both our body and our mind and allow our mind to come to rest naturally on the object of meditation. However, here too we still need the faculty of alertness, so we "plant the watch-person of mindfulness" which means we establish the faculty of mindfulness such that even though we are relaxed we do not become distracted. This second technique of relaxation should be practiced for somewhat longer sessions or intervals than the first.

The third technique is reversal. Reversal is to take an approach that is the opposite of our usual one. Normally in the context of the mahamudra practice we want to somehow avoid the arising of thoughts and therefore we are constantly trying to pacify thoughts; we are always hoping for a state in which there will be no thought. The technique of reversal is to reverse this process. Instead of attempting to stop thoughts, we almost want to instigate thoughts. We take great delight in the arising of thoughts and allow ourselves to become very disappointed when thoughts do not arise. We maintain the degree of mindfulness and alertness necessary to recognize the arising of thoughts, but when thoughts do arise we take delight in them. We think, the more the better, and when they do not arise we experience some disappointment. Ironically, this will cause thoughts not to arise and will allow us to arrest our mind in a very natural and relaxed way.

Next in the text, the distinction is made between the near experience of stillness in the mind and the actual development of the state of shamatha. It is possible from time to time, of course, that our mind will simply, for whatever reason or under whatever circumstance, be at rest. This is similar to the state of shamatha, but is not itself the achievement of stable shamatha. The state of shamatha that we are attempting to achieve through practice is one in which, while there are no thoughts arising in the mind, nevertheless there is unimpeded lucidity or clarity of the mind's cognitive capacity. In that state, the mind is so relaxed that the placement of our mind on any chosen object is easy and very workable. This state which can definitely be attained does have to be cultivated, it specifically has the characteristic of clarity and is really what is meant by shamatha.

Questions

Question: Rinpoche, I'm a little bit confused about the position of the arms when the palms are downward on the backs of the thighs behind the knees.

Thrangu Rinpoche: In the case of the posture where the hands are palms down on the thighs behind the knees, it's simply to straighten the elbows rather than allowing the elbows to sink downward. The effort involved in straightening the elbows does accomplish what is necessary here, which is promotion of clarity.

Question: With regard to the gaze, what is meant by four finger widths away from the tip of the nose? Does it mean directly in front, or below; and does it mean that we have to focus on a particular spot in space, in which case isn't there a danger of crossing the eyes?

Rinpoche: The direction, first of all, is four finger widths in front of the nose, and it indicates the direction of your gaze, not the distance of your gaze. The reason why it's four finger widths in front of your nose is so that you don't look too far downward, so that you look in that direction at that angle. How far your gaze extends is irrelevant. It's okay to look some feet in front of you. The point is that the direction of the gaze is slightly downward.

Question: In the practice of contemplating the three syllables, or later, the three spheres, are they to be visualized simultaneously, or consecutively? And a question just for the translator, could you repeat the elements, shapes, and colors slowly?

Rinpoche: With regard to the first question, if you cannot visualize them all at once, then in the beginning you can visualize them one at a time. The basic idea of the technique is that you visualize the white OM, and below that a red AH, and below that a blue HUNG. In the case of the spheres, the white one, and below that the red one, and below that the blue one—all at the same time.

Translator: Earth is a yellow square, water is a white circle, fire is a red triangle, wind is a green semi-circle, and space is a blue tetrahedron. I am sorry, I do not know any other word for tetrahedron. It is a three-sided pyramid, which is upside down with the point facing downward. The shapes get bigger, so space is the biggest, and wind is slightly smaller, fire smaller than that, and so, the smallest would be earth.

In this context, they are not visualized stacked one on top of the other; they are visualized one behind the other, so that you are looking at earth and then that dissolves into water etc. Earth is the smallest and space is the biggest. Aside from their proportional increase in size, from earth up to space, there are no specific dimensions given to them. So, you can visualize them as any size you wish. You start out with all five and then when earth dissolves into water, you only have four, and so on.

Question: Rinpoche, I just have a question concerning the three spheres of light. Do we imagine those or visualize those within the body, within our own body and the three places?

Rinpoche: Well, if you were doing this in the context of deity meditation, of course you would visualize them inside your three places. But in this context of shamatha you are working with the capacity and the tendency of your mind to look at external objects. Therefore, you visualize them in front of you.

Question: Rinpoche, we cultivate shamatha in our formal practice, but is it consistent with daily activity as well? I am not sure whether or not you are talking about mahamudra as something we can work with in our daily lives. Is that something we can do in the chaos, in all the things we have to deal with on an ordinary working basis?

Rinpoche: You can, in the sense of not entirely losing the momentum of mindfulness and alertness that is established in meditation sessions, which consists of simply not letting your mind be completely overpowered by whatever is happening; not just letting your mind run wild. Post-meditation, of course, is not true shamatha meditation, as a session of meditation can be, but there is a continuity or a momentum of the mindfulness and alertness which is cultivated in shamatha meditation.

Question: Rinpoche, my question concerns all these techniques of shamatha. Should we master all of them? Should you find one that works great and stick with that? At what point do you move on. Is it good to know them all, etc.?

Rinpoche: There is no strict requirement of either inclusiveness or sequence in your use of these techniques. In fact, this is made clear in the commentary itself. The idea of giving a variety of techniques is that through regularly using one technique of shamatha it is possible that your mind can become stale, in which case it may be appropriate to introduce another technique in order to refresh the mind. But there is no strict sequence about the order in which you use these techniques in that way, nor how much of a given technique you should use until you use another one, and so on. The deciding factor is how the technique affects your mind. It is possible that one or more of these techniques will be more beneficial for you in your own experience than the others, in which case you should concentrate on the ones that work the best.

Question: Rinpoche, could you say a little bit more about the technique of tension. What is meant by tightening awareness and body?

Rinpoche: Tension in this context means, with regard to the body, that you actually tighten your muscles, you actually exert some vigor so that your body becomes tight.[29] And while you are doing that you toughen or tighten your attitude. You strengthen the resolve not to become distracted no matter what happens. Then alternatively, relaxation consists of a corresponding relaxation of the muscles, and so on of the body, and allowing the mind to rest naturally on the technique, rather than through the force of your intention.

4 VIPASHYANA (INSIGHT) MEDITATION

SHAMATHA MEDITATION is extremely important, especially at the beginning, because we are utterly overpowered by thoughts, even though we wish to have control over our thoughts. We are utterly overpowered by our disturbing emotions, even though we wish to have control over these kleshas. Without shamatha we have no power or freedom to generate the states of mind such as virtuous states of mind that we wish to generate. We have no peace or stability of mind whatsoever. Through the practice of shamatha meditation, however, we can gradually assume control over thoughts and disturbing emotions, and we can accomplish a state of mental freedom.

Before discussing vipashyana it is important to remember, that until someone has gained a state of stable shamatha, it is necessary to continue to emphasize the development of shamatha as the basis for vipashyana realization. Even after you have developed a stable attainment of shamatha, it is necessary to maintain the continuity of that shamatha state as a basis for the practice of vipashyana. Vipashyana is the path that leads to the recognition of the mind's nature and, therefore, to freedom from the kleshas and to the attainment of supreme siddhi. Nevertheless, vipashyana, practiced in the absence of shamatha, is not very powerful.

The Approaches of Sutra and Secret Mantra

After we establish the practice of shamatha, we can begin the practice of vipashyana meditation. The reason why vipashyana is necessary to practice is that we undergo a variety of experiences, including the experience of what are perceived as external appearances and the experiences of mental events or inner states, such as mental pleasure, mental suffering, and the various emotions. All inner and outer experiences, without exception, are the confused projections of our mind. These phenomena only appear, they do not exist as we believe they do. To attain enlightenment, it is necessary to have a direct realization of their non-existence. To enable practitioners to accomplish this,

51

the Buddha gave various teachings by turning the various wheels of dharma. Essentially his teachings consist of two styles, which we call the sutra and the secret mantra teachings.

Both the sutra and mantra (or tantra) traditions were taught by the Buddha. The sutra teachings consist of a vast body of teachings traditionally classified as 84,000 different collections of dharma; but if we look at them as whole, the main idea presented in the sutra teachings is selflessness, or the emptiness of self. The Buddha presented these teachings gradually and in different stages. His initial presentation, or the first turning of the wheel of dharma, is the presentation of the Four Noble Truths. The essence of this first phase of his teaching is the non-existence of the imputed "self" of persons.

What the Buddha was addressing here is the innate fixation that we all have on the belief in a personal self. This is to say that we all believe that we exist as true personal selves, and this fixation is innate in the sense that it is not acquired through any learning process; we are born with it. On the basis of this innate assumption of an "I," we generate the idea of "other"; on the basis of the interaction between the two, we generate attachment and aversion, and this causes us to experience a great deal of pain. If there were a true self, then this attitude would be correct and there would be nothing we could do about it. But, in fact, there is no such thing as a true personal self. Since this attitude is incorrect, it can be corrected. To do this, the Buddha presented the practice of meditation upon the selflessness of the individual.

We cannot get rid of suffering by saying, "I will not suffer." We cannot eliminate attachment by saying, "I will not be attached to anything," nor eliminate aggression by saying, "I will never become angry." Yet, we do want to get rid of suffering and the disturbing emotions that are the immediate cause of suffering. The Buddha taught that to eliminate these states, which are really the results of the primary confusion of our belief in a personal self, we must get rid of the fundamental cause. But we cannot simply say, "I will not believe in the personal self." The only way to eliminate suffering is to actually recognize the experience of a self as a misconception, which we do by proving directly to ourselves that there is no such personal self. We must actually realise this. Once we do, then automatically the misconception of a self and our fixation on that "self" will disappear. Only by directly experiencing selflessness can we end the process of confused projection. This is why the Buddha emphasized meditation on selflessness or egolessness. However, to meditate on egolessness, we must undertake a process that begins with a conceptual understanding of egolessness; then, based on that understanding, there can be meditation, and finally realization.

The Buddha presented a great deal of evidence for the non-existence of a personal self. To simplify this whole concept, essentially there are two fixations that we are attempting to rectify here. One is the fixation on "I," the imputed self, and the other is the fixation on "mine," that which we regard as belonging to or pertaining to that imputed self. Because it's easier to begin by attacking the second of these concepts first, we'll look at this "mine."

For example, if I go into a watch store and while I'm there another person who is looking at the watches drops one on the ground and breaks it, I see this happen, I am fully aware that a watch has broken, but I experience no pain. If, on the other hand, I am handling my own watch, and I drop it on the ground, and it breaks, I experience pain. Why should I react so differently to fundamentally identical events? The reason I react differently is that, in the second instance, I have generated the concept "mine" about this watch. I have imputed the fact that this watch pertains to myself. Now, if we examine this imputation, we discover that it is a mere belief, on which we generate an unnecessary fixation. There is nothing inside or outside the watch that is a "mine." Therefore, "mine" isn't anywhere. It is unnecessary therefore to fixate on it and suffer on that account. Through this kind of rigorous analysis, we can determine that there is nothing we can call "mine."

We generate a great deal of suffering through this imputation of "mine," which we affix to a large body of things such as "my neighbourhood," "my race," or "my country." But none of these things are inherently "mine," we merely designate them as such.

The root of the belief in "mine" is, of course, the false belief in "I," or the personal self as applied to our own imputed selves. The first question we have to ask is, where exactly is this "I"? When we scrutinize all of the things that we think might be this "I," we can't find it anywhere. The way the Buddha presented this was through the idea of aggregates; that which we think of as "I" is, in fact, made up of several things, each of which is an aggregate or heap of many elements. Generally speaking, we have a body and a mind, and our body, which is called the aggregate of form, is made up of many, many parts; it's infinitely divisible. Then our mind consists of sensations, perceptions, thoughts, consciousness, and so on, and each of these can also be divided and further subdivided and so on. The point of this type of analysis is to understand that we are not a unit that can meaningfully be called "I" as a singular, discrete, or separate entity.

Furthermore, there is a problem with determining what to designate as "I." We assume that there is "I" and there is "mine," and these are somehow distinct, and yet the distinction between the two does not hold up when we look at how we make it. For example, we commonly think and say "my body." Well, if "my body" is "mine," then it is not an "I"; it's something that pertains to or belongs to the "I." If that's the case, then the "I" is probably the mind, since the body is something possessed by the "I." Yet sometimes, we think "my mind," in which case the mind, at that moment, can't be the "I," because it is clearly seen to be a possession of the "I," in which case, the "I" must be the body. But before, the "I" was the mind, and the body was its possession. Now the situation is reversed. How is this possible? Let us assume, for the moment, that the "I" is the body. But then we think, "My head hurts." Well, obviously, the "I" must be the body but not the head. Then we think, "My hand hurts." In that case, it's not the hand, either.

If you follow this reasoning, you will discover that there's no clear distinction, practically speaking, between the bases of designation for the concepts "I" and "mine." Some things we sometimes designate as "I," at other times we designate them as "mine." This is because "I" is sometimes held to be both our body and our mind, at other times it's just our body or just our mind, and sometimes it's just part of the body. The reason for this inconsistency is that there is no true basis for this designation in the first place. It is a mere imputation. After you recognize this through logical analysis, then on that basis you can proceed with meditation and come to a definitive realization. It was for this purpose that the Buddha presented the doctrine of the emptiness of self.

In further teachings, the Buddha presented what is called the emptiness of outer phenomena; the emptiness of things. He primarily presented the teachings on emptiness in sutras on the perfection of knowledge, the Prajnaparamita teachings. There are many such teachings classified into long sutras, medium sutras, short sutras, and very short sutras. The one that we usually rely on is the shortest of these, called *The Essence of the Perfection of Knowledge*, more commonly known as the *Heart Sutra*. This sutra makes the statement, "There are no eyes, no ears, no nose, no tongue, no body; there is no form, no sound, no smell, no taste, no touch." What is being pointed out here is that the various appearances we experience have no inherent existence. If the things we experience actually had an inherent existence as we believe them to have, we could not say that they were empty; we could not say, "No eyes, no ears," and so on. The Buddha, though, realized the emptiness of all phenomena. We begin with the Buddha's statement and proceed to study and analyze and come to an understanding of what it means. Then, on the basis of that understanding, we meditate on it, and finally, on the basis of that meditation, we develop a direct realization of this emptiness of all things.

In the Buddha's actual presentation of emptiness, he made statements such as, "There are no eyes, no ears," and so on, which indicates the non-existence of things that we perceive. He did not clearly explain either what he meant or the reasons for making this statement. The reason why he didn't give a lot of explanation on emptiness was that the people he was teaching at that time were extremely intelligent and diligent and perceived it right away. Eventually, after the Buddha's time, people could not simply read the statement, "There are no eyes," and understand what he really meant. So it became necessary for a further explanation, at which time great teachers such as Nagarjuna, Chandrakirti, Asanga, and others began to compose lucid expositions of what the Buddha was trying to convey in his initial presentations of emptiness. Contained in these commentators' explanations are logical arguments giving reasons why it is necessary to accept the emptiness of all phenomena. When we initially hear or read the statement, "All things are empty," it's almost impossible to understand what this really means. But when we, in a rigorous and systematic fashion, study these explanations of the Buddha's teachings on emptiness, which are generally called the Middle Way teachings, then we can come to a decisive ascertainment of what the Buddha meant.

To illustrate these logical arguments simply, take my hand. Now, my hand is really my hand, I can see it, I can be aware of it in various ways, it has all of the characteristics of a hand, and it performs the function of a hand. So it's entirely reasonable to call my hand, "my hand." Yet, when I actually scrutinize my hand, I cannot find it anywhere. Because if I look at each and every part of the hand, no one part of it, at any level, is actually the hand. On a gross level if we look at the hand, first we see the thumb. The thumb is not a hand, it's merely a thumb. A forefinger is not a hand, it's merely a forefinger. A middle finger is not a hand, it's a middle finger. A ring finger is merely a ring finger, and the little finger is merely that. Or, if we want to go by the materials of which it's composed, the skin is not my hand, the flesh is not my hand, the bones are not my hand, and the marrow within those bones is not my hand. My hand is no one of these things, each of which can, of course, be further subdivided. The point of this is that my hand is not one thing. "Hand," or "my hand" to be specific, is a label that we affix on an aggregate, and it is a mere name for an arbitrarily isolated aggregate of things.

We might think, "Okay, so there's no hand, but there are fingers." But if we take any one of the fingers, then we have the same problem. Because if we look at a finger and ask, "Where is the finger?" We find it's not the first joint, it's not the second joint, it's not the third joint, it's not the nail, and so on. So just as, on a coarse level, there was no hand, on a more subtle level, there are no fingers, because each one of the fingers is, again, merely a name, merely a concept that we affix to an arbitrary isolation of things.

Now, if we move from merely considering my hand, and consider me as a whole, we see something that we designate as Thrangu Tulku sitting on something that we designate as a throne. And yet, just as we've determined that my right hand does not exist, we must also accept that my left hand does not exist. My feet are the same sort of thing and my head as well, and in fact I cannot be said to really exist. Well, when you look, you see something, and yet what you see and what you designate on the basis of what you see are not truly there. All things are like that; that is what the Buddha meant when he said, "No eyes, no ears, no tongue, no nose."

The approach in the sutras then is to develop a conceptual understanding of emptiness and gradually refine that understanding through meditation, which eventually produces a direct experience of emptiness. This approach is very clear, in so far as conceptual understanding is concerned; there is a very clear presentation of the meaning of emptiness. It's very easy to understand this. At the same time, however, it is very hard to actually meditate upon this, because we are proceeding from a conceptual understanding produced by analysis and logical inference into a direct experience to generate certainty about emptiness. Because we have from the beginning taken inferential reasoning as the basis of our ascertainment, this takes a great deal of time. It is because of this that in the sutras, the Buddha said that to attain Buddhahood takes three periods of incalculable numbers of eons of gathering the accumulations. The reason it takes so long is that we are essentially taking inferential reasoning as our method or as the path. Now, is it necessary for us to undertake such a long and arduous path? It's acceptable to do so, but there is an alternative, which is the other approach, that which the Buddha taught in the tantras and which was utilized and propagated by the great siddhas.

The Buddha declared that through the practice of the tantric approach, full Buddhahood could be attained in one lifetime and one body. This was the approach taken by the great mahasiddhas who meditated and realized the meaning and attained siddhi in their lifetimes. The instructions for doing this are the instructions of Vajrayana meditation. The primary difference between the sutra approach and the approach of Vajrayana (secret mantra or tantra) is that in the sutra approach, we take inferential reasoning as our path and in the Vajrayana approach, we take direct experience as our path. In the Vajrayana we are cultivating simple, direct experiencing or "looking." We do this primarily by simply looking directly at our own mind. Both external appearances and our mind are empty in fundamentally the same way. The difference, however, is that external appearances are not obviously empty, so attempting to ascertain the emptiness of external appearances requires us to fall back on analysis and inference, the sutra approach. But when we're working directly with our own mind, which is obviously, utterly empty, we have no need for any kind of analysis whatsoever because it is very easy to directly experience our mind's inherent emptiness.

Looking at the Mind

The technique of looking directly at our mind and our own experience is what is referred to in our tradition as insight or vipashyana meditation. In *Pointing Out the Dharmakaya* ten methods of the practice of vipashyana are given. There are two aspects: viewing or looking at the mind, and a corresponding introduction to or pointing out of the nature of mind. Each of these has five sections.

Looking at Stillness	Pointing Out the Mind in Stillness
Looking at Occurrence	Pointing Out the Mind in Occurrence
Looking at Appearances	Pointing Out the Mind within Appearances
Looking at the Body and Mind as the Same or Different	Pointing Out the Body and Mind as the Same or Different
Looking at Stillness and Occurrence as the Same or Different	Pointing Out Stillness and Occurrence as the Same or Different

These are all the ways of looking at your mind. But first of all, we need to understand that looking at something and analyzing something are quite different. Analysis is not really meditation; it is a conceptual process of inferential reasoning. "Looking," as we're using it here, means looking simply and directly at what we are experiencing. It does not mean thinking about it or attempting to analyze it, or attempting to speculate about what it might be. It does not mean entertaining questions such as, "What is the nature of mind like?" It does not mean attempting to tell yourself what it should be like. You should not, in this practice, generate the idea that there is nothing to see, and that therefore the mind must be utterly insubstantial, and so on. In the context of this practice you are simply trying to directly experience your mind as it is without the overlay of conceptual expectations or ideas.

Looking at Stillness

Among the various methods of looking at the mind presented in this text, the first of the five ways is looking at the mind within stillness, which begins with the practice of shamatha. Through the practice of shamatha we come to experience the cessation of coarse thoughts and a peaceful and calm state of mind. The practice of looking at the mind within stillness consists of looking at the nature of that experience of stillness or shamatha.

The first prerequisite for this technique is taking a physical posture appropriate for the meditation, which is usually the meditation posture known as the seven dharmas of Vairochana. In the specific context of vipashyana, the gaze is particularly important. Here the gaze is not the same as the usual gaze for shamatha, which is lowered. Here the gaze is somewhat upraised. You look straight forward, but slightly upward, neither looking to the left nor to the right. Then, taking that posture and adopting that gaze, you relax your mind into the state of shamatha, retaining the faculties of mindfulness and alertness so that you are not overpowered by thoughts. Allowing your mind to relax and rest naturally in shamatha in this way, you are then free from the defects of torpor and excitement. Because you are not distracted by the presence of thoughts, your mind is not scattered, distracted, or excited. Although your mind is at peace there is no blankness or obscurity to it. Your mind is not torpid or sunken. In order to maintain that state of shamatha, in which your mind is neither torpid nor agitated, you need to maintain some degree of mindfulness.

When your mind is at rest in that way, you will have an experience of what it is like when your mind is in a state of tranquility. There will be an actual experience of that tranquility. Within that experience, try to see or look directly at the nature of that mind which is generating that tranquility or stillness.

With regard to our experience, in the traditional vocabulary of dharma we would call what we experience a relative truth, produced through interdependence, and we would call the nature itself an absolute truth. In our ordinary experience of the mind, it seems to us that the mind does exist. We have a distinct experience of stillness, and therefore we tend to think that stillness exists as a state. And when the mind is not still, but is agitated and thoughts are arising, we tend to think that thoughts — since we seem to experience them — actually do exist. This is so because, not having looked at the mind, we are generating assumptions based upon what seems to be the case in our experience. There is a certain validity to the evidence of experience, because we do experience whatever we do experience. Nevertheless, the state of stillness that we experience in shamatha is produced by the cause and conditions of our cultivation of shamatha itself. In order to determine, however, what the true nature of that state is, we need to look at that which is still, at that which is at rest, which is to say, at our mind.

Questions for Looking at the Mind within Stillness

As part of the traditional process of learning these techniques of looking at the mind, various questions were posed to the student. Originally, as I mentioned before, this kind of teaching was transmitted in an oral lineage, and in earlier times, none of the material was ever written down. A teacher would practice until he or she realized mahamudra, and then, when teaching his or her students, would use various questions to examine the student's experience. In response to the student's answers, the teacher would give further instruction as appropriate

Now, this style of passing on the teachings, which is called an oral or hearing lineage, is an excellent way of guiding practitioners. However, because nothing is written down, there is the danger that the instructions and therefore the lineage will be lost. Because of this danger, the teachings were written down during the time of the Ninth Gyalwang Karmapa, Wangchuk Dorje, in books like the text we're following which was actually written by Wangchuk Dorje. Certain teachers have voiced an objection to this practice, saying it's inappropriate to write down the oral instructions, because then they become a book that people can just read without receiving the instructions in the sequential and methodical fashion that was originally intended. This may be true, but the danger of the instructions being lost forever far outweighs the danger of people misusing the text.

When the instructions had not yet been written down, the teacher posed the questions privately to the student. Although now they're much more standardised because of being written down, so, we will begin to look at the questions.

Seven Questions

The first technique of looking at the mind within stillness, involves seven questions. The first of these questions is: When you look at that which is still or at rest—does it have a form or not? That is to say, does it have substantial characteristics or not? If it has a form, then it must have some kind of shape. If it has a shape, what shape does it have? If it does not have a form and therefore has no shape, what characteristics does it have? Now, do not say that you cannot see it or cannot detect it, because after all this is just your mind. It is right there. If it has a form, if it has a shape, if it has any substantial characteristic, you will see it.

We experience something. Therefore, if there is something, something must have started it at some point. And it must abide somehow and somewhere, and, it if it comes to an end, it must come to an end in some particular way, in some particular place. Well then, since you have an experience of your mind, which seems to be something, look to see; does the mind start anywhere? Does it abide anywhere? Does it end anywhere? If the mind starts somewhere, then where does it start? How does it start? By mind here, we mean what you can call mind or thought. So when we are talking about the starting of mind we mean the arising of thought. We have the experience of the presence of thoughts. Well, at a certain point these thoughts come into presence or arise. How do they arise? Do they arise somewhere? And what do they arise from? And then while thoughts are present, while they abide, where do they abide? How do they abide? What does it mean that they abide? When thoughts disappear, do they actually end or cease? If so, where and how? What exactly does this disappearance of thoughts consist of? In particular, when you are looking at the mind you can look at it both in a state of stillness or rest, and in the presence or emergence of thoughts. In both cases you look for, and see if you can see, an origin, a location, and a destination. For example, when the mind is still or at rest, is it inside or outside of your body? What is it like? And when thoughts arise, do they arise inside your body and, if so, where? Or do they arise outside your body and, if so, where, and exactly what is it that arises when we say, thoughts arise.

If you keep on looking at your mind in this way, without being satisfied by a mere idea or estimation of how you think that mind is, if you keep on looking at it until you have a decisive and direct experience of it, that is the first part of looking at the mind within stillness.

The second question, still within the same section, is, when the mind is within stillness, look directly at it and see if it has any kind of substantial characteristics whatsoever, such as location, such as shape, [size, colour, etc.] and so forth.

People can have different kinds of experiences when they are looking at the mind. Some people have the kind of experience where they think that there is nothing there whatsoever, where the mind in a state of stillness is like the horns of a rabbit. It does not exist anywhere, neither inside nor outside the body, and therefore it has no substantial characteristics: no color, no shape, no location, and so on. You should look to see if this really is what you experience. That looking to see if you find nothing whatsoever is the third question.

The fourth question or the fourth way of looking is concerned with another type of experience that people sometimes have, which is that, when they are practicing shamatha, and within that shamatha, when they are looking at the mind that is still or at rest, they look for it and they do not have the experience of there being nothing whatsoever. The fact that there is a state of cognitive lucidity or mere clarity that is definitely present in the sense that there is a capacity to know, but that, on the other hand, cannot be said to be something or nothing, should cause you to look to see if that is what you experience.

While in the experience described in the fourth way of looking there is a predominance of cognitive lucidity, here, in the fifth way of looking, you actually experience an absence of any kind of conceptually classifiable things, such as anything good or bad, or even the presence or absence of clarity. In fact, you experience an absence of awareness altogether. What you experience is an obscurity, somewhat like darkness, except that it is not a visual experience, but an experience of utter bewilderment. You should look to see if this is what you experience.

The sixth way of looking is that some people, when they are looking at their mind in this way, experience the presence of something definite, something that they can see and clearly detect. You should look to see if you experience that.

The seventh question is concerned with yet another type of experience that you might have when looking at the mind, which is an instance of what Gampopa called, "confusing understanding and experience." This is a situation in which, while you are meditating, the ideas you have absorbed about the mind in your study arise as thoughts, and you confuse these ideas or concepts with experience of the mind. For example, you might have heard that the mind transcends existence and non-existence, and so on, and that arises in your mind and you think that that conceptual understanding is an actual experience. The conceptual understanding of these ideas is good, not bad, but it is called a dry understanding, because it cannot grow into or lead to any result. Such a dry understanding cannot produce the increasing of experience, cannot produce the attainment of wisdom or the eradication of the kleshas.

A related situation is when you have absorbed various ideas and terminology of dharma, such as the exalted notion of emptiness and so on, and you use these concepts to fabricate experience, when you try to talk yourself into the experience of the mind as emptiness, or as lucidity,[30] or as the unity of lucidity and emptiness, or as inexpressible, and so on, which are all things which you have heard or learned. But even though you may convince yourself that you have experienced things you have not, and then may recount these experiences to others in exalted technical jargon, this will be of no benefit to you or to others, and will really only deceive you. Rather than doing that, you should simply look directly at the mind and see it as it is without any kind of presupposition based upon learning.

The View of Direct Experience

The essence of Buddhadharma, the special feature of the Buddha's teaching, which is particularly emphasized in the common vehicle but runs through all his teachings, is the selflessness of persons. As is taught, it is through the recognition of the selflessness of persons that one can attain the state of an arhat.[31] Therefore, this remains the essence of our meditation practice. With regard to the basis on which we impute the existence of this supposed but spurious self of persons, while sometimes it is our bodies, more commonly or usually it is our mind. We impute the existence of a self of persons on the basis of our misperception of the mind as being real and substantial, and therefore, fit to be regarded as a self. But when you do this practice and look at the mind, even though we may have the habit of regarding the mind as substantial, you will see that the mind is without any substantial character-istics whatsoever, which means that, through recognizing the insubstantial-ity of the basis for the imputation of the self of persons, you therefore recognize the selflessness of persons automatically.

Although we regard the realization of the selflessness of persons as some-thing particularly exalted and therefore difficult to achieve, in fact, if you look directly at your mind and see its nature, you will realize this selflessness. This is not a matter of trying to convince yourself that there is no self in the mind. It is simply a matter of looking. And when you look, you will see that there is no mind, and that therefore there is no self that could be imputed on the basis of the mind.

In the specific context of the Mahayana, both in the Mahayana sutras in general and, in particular, in the Prajnaparamita sutras, the Buddha princi-pally taught that all dharmas, all things without exception, are empty. We normally determine this emptiness of all things through the reasonings of the Madhyamaka school, through which we can come to a conceptual under-standing that everything is emptiness. But this understanding is really just a thought or an idea that we come upon at the end of a period of analysis. It is still not a direct experience of emptiness at all. In contrast, the instruction of the siddhas of the past has been simply to look directly at your mind. While we tend to think that the mind exists and is something substantial, when you look at it, you discover it is nowhere inside or outside your body, or anywhere in between. By simply looking directly at your mind without any kind of presuppositions, you will discover emptiness as the mind's nature, and discovering it directly in that way, not having to look at things outside of yourself, not having to resort to analysis or logical reasoning, you will wonder, "Why have I not realized this before?"

Through meditation, when you look directly at the mind's nature, you can come to have direct experience of the mind's nature, which is, in a sense, easy. But in order to do this, you need to avoid what is called, "sewing on the patch of concepts," which is the attempt to control or alter what you are experiencing in your meditation through the application of various concepts such as emptiness, and so forth. You might say that the mind must be empty, so I am going to discover emptiness, or it must be lucid, so I am going to discover cognitive lucidity, and so on. In general, of course, these ideas are not bad, but they are not appropriate in the context of meditation, simply because they do not lead to realization, since they themselves are divorced from direct experience. Far more profitable is to look directly at the mind without any kind of ideas about it, within the state of stillness produced by shamatha practice. In that way, viewing the mind directly, you have no need to imagine anything about it or to fabricate any kind of state or experience. You have no need to pretend that that which does not seem empty to you is empty, that that which does not seem clear to you is clear, or that that which does not seem to be a union of lucidity and emptiness is such a union. In short, if you look directly at the mind, you will experience its nature directly without conceptual overlay.

Some people are discouraged when, contrary to their expectation, they initially have no decisive determination of the mind's nature. But when you are looking at the mind directly, you are seeing its nature, which you can call emptiness or selflessness or whatever. You simply need to keep on looking at it. There is nothing else that needs to be done. It is best to look at it, and then, when your mind starts to become fatigued, to rest, and then to go back to looking at the mind and then to rest, and so on. If you keep on looking in this way until you actually gain a decisive and direct experience of the mind's nature, you will gain it. In short, avoid the situation of becoming discouraged — thinking, "I will never be able to recognize this" — and avoid the situation of attempting to fabricate experience through the application of concepts and theories, and continue to look directly at the mind very simply and without presuppositions. Then protect that experience by simply allowing whatever experience arises to continue. This way of looking at the mind, or viewing the mind directly without concepts, is called the direct view, or the view of direct experience. I am going to stop here, if you have any questions you are welcome to ask them.

Questions

Question: Rinpoche, those who watch the forest in the summertime know that smoke is often evidence of fire, and further, those who study the phenomenon of electricity comprehend that light in a light bulb is evidence of electricity. So, my question is: Maybe that which looks at the nature of the mind isn't really powerful enough or insightful enough. Modern science, when it has use of very sophisticated technology, can see that someone with Alzheimer's mind is different from a person who does not have Alzheimer's. So, there are differences between qualities of mind. So, I am curious; does this scientific evidence somehow contradict what you are saying?

Thrangu Rinpoche: There seem to be two questions here, so we will treat them separately. The first is about the use of reasoning from results to causes, as in determining the existence of a fire through the presence of smoke, which is its result. Reasoning from results to causes is one of the varieties of reasonings used in inferential valid cognition. In general, there are two types of valid cognition that we might use in determining the nature of mind. One is inferential valid cognition and the other is direct valid cognition. The choice you make in determining which type of valid cognition to apply depends on the thing to which you are applying it. It is appropriate, and indeed necessary, to use inferential valid cognition if investigating what is called a hidden thing. A hidden thing is something that you cannot know directly, like a fire that you cannot physically see, so you must determine its existence by the presence of smoke, which can be seen. In the case of something that is hidden, you need inferential valid cognition to determine its existence or absence. But in the case of the opposite type of thing, called an evident thing, you have no need to apply inference, since you can use direct valid cognition or direct experience. For example, I do not need to infer the presence of a bell on the table in front of me, since I can see it. I do not need to speculate about what possible evidence the bell might have left of its presence since it is right in front of me. I do not need to reasoning at all. Now, with regard to meditation on the mind's nature, the mind is not a hidden thing; it is an evident thing. It is your mind. Therefore, you can know it directly and experience its nature directly, and for that reason it is not necessary to use inferential valid cognition in determining the mind's nature.

The second question is about the difference in the mind of those whose brains have been damaged by illness, as opposed to those whose brains have not been damaged in that way. Of course, damage to the brain will change the way your mind manifests. We do not even need to look as far in as the brain.

If you have a defect in your eyes, the organ of vision, then there will naturally be a reduction in your ability to see form, since the organ of the eye is the principal condition for the physical perception of form. In fact, we could even say that if you merely press your eyes, you will see double, so therefore, any change in the physical body that connects with your six consciousnesses or six groups, will affect their functioning. However, while a change in someone's brain may affect the clarity of their cognition or the manifestation of their mind, it does not affect the nature of their mind, which remains the same.

Question: You mentioned, Rinpoche, that one can use either direct cognition or inferential valid cognition as two ways of reasoning, and that it is unnecessary to use inferential valid cognition with those things that one obviously can see, like the bell in front of you. And it is only valid to use inferential valid cognition for those things which are hidden. Where does the supposition come from that the nature of the mind is self-evident, as is the bell in front of you? Are there not qualities of the mind that perhaps are hidden to that which watches the mind or observes the mind, and should one not, therefore, use inferential valid cognition?

Rinpoche: The reason why your mind is an evident thing and not hidden is that it is your mind. Therefore, it is right where you are. A hidden thing is by definition hidden by something in between the viewer and the thing itself. For example, a sound that cannot be directly heard because it is too low, or something that cannot be seen because it is too small or too far away, or because there is something in between you and it. Your mind is right where you are; there is nothing in between your mind and your mind. With regard to the appropriateness of the bell as an example, in fact, the mind is just as evident as the bell. The bell is right there and we can all see it, but we have to look at it. The mind is right there and everyone can see it, but they have to look at it. The reason that we do not see our mind is that we avoid looking at it. We look outwards away from the mind. We go to great lengths not to look at the mind. So, just as if I were to turn myself away from the bell so that it were not in my line of vision and therefore I could not see it, in the same way, until we are brought to the point where we look at the mind, the mind is, so to speak, out of our line of vision.

Question: Rinpoche, I think it was your sixth or seventh point; it was after the lucidity. I think you said, "At this point you will see something, you will see a thing, or you will see something." Could you explain that, or elaborate on that. I didn't quite understand that.

Rinpoche: The sixth point is about one of the types of experiences that you might have as you are looking at the mind. You get the idea that there is something really there. There seems to be something to apprehend, something to get hold of, and it is in contrast to the previous point, which was describing a related but somewhat opposite experience, where you get the idea that there is nothing there. These are describing different sorts of experiences that one might have while looking at the mind. And the description of the experiences themselves is a description of what you experience, in the beginning, as you look. You need to go further in order to have an actual realization of it. This is basically just a sense of there being something there, it is obviously not something physical or something you could get hold of with your hand. But it is a feeling or an experience that there is something—that the mind is something, a thing.

What is your experience?

Same questioner: Well, it shifts back and forth.

Rinpoche: Between what and what?

Same questioner: There is a sense of having a slight experience of most of these.

Rinpoche: Then keep on looking and that will help.

Question: Rinpoche, there are some people who believe that many of the tantric practices and the practice of looking at your mind and developing insight and clarity will lead to psychic abilities, the development of psychic abilities. Could you address that? What is the general view on seeking out advice from psychics, or the Buddhist view of that whole thing of developing psychic abilities, and the ability to channel yidams, and all that? Is this to be encouraged? Is it beneficial, and in general, what is the Buddhist view on it?

Rinpoche: I do not know how to answer that question. [laughter]

Question: Rinpoche, for someone like me, who has an enormous amount of obscuration, I find it very difficult to visualize, and usually by the time a sadhana such as that of Guru Rinpoche is finished, I am still on the protection circle. I am wondering if there is a subtle difference between, or a major difference, maybe, between visualization and imagination?

Rinpoche: Essentially, visualization and imagination are similar. The basic idea is that one of the ways we think is in imagery. So, if you think about someone or something intensely enough, then your thoughts will not only appear as linguistic thoughts, but actually as images. This happens to us naturally all the time. Whenever we think with some intensity about a place, or about people, friends, or enemies, then we get visual images of them in our mind, and this is, in fact, a visualization. The key is to understand that if you try too hard to visualize something or someone it will not work. On the other hand, if you relax, then when you are meditating upon Guru Rinpoche, for example, the image will definitely appear over time. In order to understand how relaxation and the intensity of thought function together to produce the image of the visualization, you might actually try thinking about your home, or thinking about people you know, and see how it happens that these images arise in your mind. Then use the same approach to generate the iconographic images in visualization practice.

Question: Rinpoche, recently I've been having an experience of there being something just in the back of my mind, just out of reach, something that seems to be quite significant, quite immense, even brightness involved or whatever. But it is something that's just beyond my reach, just outside of my perception. I am wondering how I should approach this? Should I approach it as an illusion and ignore it? Or should I pursue it as an object of meditation and try to perceive what is just my consciousness, or what?

Rinpoche: You are probably better off just letting it alone, because often those things that seem to be at the back of our mind, that we just cannot quite grasp, are the emergence of very, very old, or long-standing habits. And if you succeed in bringing them into consciousness, they are usually not of much use anyway. So you are probably better off just leaving it alone.

Question: Rinpoche, when I observe my own mind, I notice that it is indeed without form, without color, without location inside or outside my body. I accept that as true, I've looked, and that is a fact. But what I am trying to reconcile is the Buddhist theory of mind with various other theories of mind that are emerging in the scientific age. And these are the kinds of questions I am posing to you. Your statement that because it is your mind, it cannot be hidden, is a supposition, and it is based on a supposition that because it is yours it cannot be hidden. And that's not necessarily true. There are many things that are mine, my blood vessels, my genes that are mine, but they're hidden to me, they're hidden to my powers of mental capacity. My question is this then: There is a Buddhist theory with respect to the nature of mind, and then there is cognitive science which is trying to study the mind as an object. Scientists are using various sophisticated machinery, and they look at the mind as an object, and they see color, and they see magnetic resonance. They see that there are other qualities, because they are looking with a more powerful tool of observation. So this is the question I am asking Rinpoche: How do you reconcile, in a sense, the Buddhist theory of the nature of mind, not just the samsaric mind, with other kind of theories that are looking at the mind as an object with scientific tools, to determine what its nature is?

Rinpoche: The contents and parts of your body that are within your body cannot be seen by you directly for two reasons: one is that on a coarse level they are within your body, they are covered by your skin; so unless you actually rip open your chest, and so on, you will not see your own intestines. In that case, the body is hidden from you because there is something in between your viewing organ, which is the eye, and what you are looking at. But there is nothing in between the object, which is the mind's nature, and the organ which views it, which is that mind itself. The mind's nature is not covered by any layer of skin or covering that impedes itself from seeing itself. It is, itself, looking at itself, and therefore it can see itself. The other reason which you brought up, why you cannot see various things in your body—such as the DNA and so on—is their subtlety, or how small they are. Because there are many things in our bodies that are extremely tiny, then we need, as you say, various machines in order to be able to see them. But the mind is not tiny like that. The mind is not a tiny subtle particle that needs to be viewed with electron microscopes, or whatever. The only reason we do not see the mind is that the mind itself is turned outward away from itself, it looks outside and therefore sees everything but itself. We could not, by attempting to look outward in that way, see the mind. Therefore, no machine, no matter how sophisticated it might be, could ever see the mind itself. When you are looking at the mind you are not trying to see something as nothing, or nothing as something. You are just trying to see it as it is.

5 THE ESSENTIAL NATURE OF MIND IN STILLNESS

So far I have talked about looking at the mind within stillness, which essentially consists of looking at the nature of the mind which is at rest in the experience of shamatha. Just as time is composed of a series of moments or instants, in the same way mind is composed of a series or a continuum of instants. Mind is generated in an instant, ceases, and is generated again in a subsequent instant, and so on. One of the implications of this is that the mind that exists at a given instant is no longer present at the second, or subsequent, instant.

Therefore, if, when we are looking at the mind, we attempt to use the mind of the second instant to look at the mind of the first instant, we are looking at the past. And what we will be doing will be looking at something that is no longer present, and therefore cannot be directly seen. We cannot use the mind of the second, third, or fourth instant to look at the mind of the first instant. We must look at the mind of the first instant with the mind of the first instant, and at the mind of the second instant with the mind of the second instant, and so on. In short, only if the looking at the mind is simultaneous with the mind that is being looked at will the viewing of the mind be direct. That is how we look at the mind.

On the basis of the five ways of looking at the mind, various experiences will arise. Specifically, we will have a genuine experience of our mind's nature. It's necessary to resolve the nature of that experience, so that we correctly and fully recognize what we are experiencing. This recognition is called ngo-drup, which means both pointing out and recognizing. In addition to the five ways of looking at the mind, the text gives a corresponding set of five ways of pointing out the mind's nature. Although the five ways of looking are to some extent quite different from one another as to technique, they all lead us to discover the same nature of mind, the same lucidity-emptiness. The five ways of pointing out the nature of mind, on the other hand, are not as different from one another.

Pointing Out Stillness

Now, we will look at the first way of pointing out, which I'm going to present in the hopes that it will help your meditation practice.

When you practice the first of the five ways of looking at the mind, what will you experience? When you are looking at your mind, will you actually see a thing? Is there a thing to discover about which you can then say, "This is the mind that I have seen?" No, there is nothing like that. Because there is no thing that we can call the mind, the Buddha talked of emptiness and self-lessness. If in fact the mind did consist of some concrete thing that we could point to and call mind, then the Buddha would not have characterized it as empty and selfless. In the terminology of philosophy, we would say that this is the absence of true existence of the mind. The point of this is that no matter how much you look at the mind, and no matter what you may expect to find, you will not find a thing of any kind. And your not finding such a thing is not because you do not know how to look at the mind, or because you are not looking hard enough; it is simply because that is how it is. There is no thing, no substantial existence within the mind. It was therefore said by the Third Gyalwa Karmapa, "It does not exist and has not been seen by any of the Victorious Ones." Because there is no substantial existence within or to the mind, then no Buddha of the past, present, or future has, does, or will see such a thing in it.

There is nothing to see when you look at the mind, but on the other hand, there is not an absolute absence of anything either. Normally, when we talk about emptiness we generate a concept of absolute nothingness, absolute non-existence, as for example, the horns of a rabbit or the emptiness of empty space. The emptiness that is the mind's nature is not like that either. It is not an absolute nothingness. For example, when you look at the mind within the context of shamatha practice, then you do not see color, shape, or any kind of substantial characteristic in that way. But that is not the discovery of an absolute nothingness, because this emptiness that is the mind's nature is not insentient. It is at the same time a cognition and a cognitive capacity, because it is, in fact, that which can and does know experience.

So from one point of view, you can't say it's merely empty, because there is cognition, but you can't say there's something there, either, because there are no substantial characteristics—no color, no shape, in fact nothing to grasp whatsoever. There is nothing you can fixate on, nothing you can label or designate accurately. Because of this, we say the mind is empty. Not only the mind, of course, but all things are empty. The reason we look at the mind is that the mind is obviously empty. Besides, the mind's emptiness can recognize itself. That's why we say it's not merely empty; its emptiness is, at the same time, a clear lucidity, a very clean lucidity. This term "lucidity" is sometimes misunderstood. It always has a connotation of light, which is often misunderstood as being a kind of visual experience of physical light. Which it is not. It's simply the cognitive lucidity of your mind.

When you look at the nature of your mind, you see that its essential nature is emptiness. But this does not make your mind nonexistent, and make your body, therefore, a corpse. For while the nature of your mind is emptiness, it also has this natural characteristic of cognitive lucidity, and in fact, this cognitive lucidity which characterizes the mind is inseparable from the emptiness which is its fundamental nature. Therefore, after saying, "It does not exist and has not been seen by any of the Victorious Ones," the Third Karmapa goes on to say, "It does not not-exist, it is the basis of samsara and nirvana." Although the mind is empty in the sense of being devoid of any kind of substantial existence, it nevertheless is the ground for all of the qualities of Buddhahood and for all of the confusion of samsara. So, you would have to say, finally, that it is beyond being something or nothing. You cannot say the mind is something because it has no substantial characteristics that make it meaningful to view it that way. Nor can you say that it is nothing, because it is the ground for all qualities and the ground of experience. Therefore, the mind is said to be beyond being something or nothing, beyond existence and non-existence. One of the implications of this is that when looking at the mind you have no need to pretend that that which exists does not exist, or that that which does not exist, does exist. You simply see the mind as it is.

When you rest in this experience of the mind, which is beyond extremes or elaborations, what is the experience of that like? It is characterized by a profound state of ease, which means an absence of agitation or discomfort. Therefore the experience is comfortable and pleasant. The term comfortable does not indicate pleasure in the sense of something you're attached to, or the pleasure of acting out an attachment or passion. It's simply the absence of any kind of discomfort or imperfection in the nature of mind itself. Therefore, the experience of that nature is characterized by comfy blissfulness. This is as close as we can come in words to what you experience when you look at your mind. You couldn't actually communicate what you experience. It's beyond expression. In fact, the Buddha said that this nature is the Prajnaparamita that is inexpressible, indescribable, and even inconceivable. If it had substantial characteristics, for example, if it had a color, at least you could say, it's blue or it's yellow or it's red. And if it either existed or it didn't, then you could say it exists or it doesn't exist. But it's beyond any of that. Therefore, you can't accurately say anything about it. Therefore, it was characterized by Marpa the Translator as being like the situation of a mute person tasting sugar. The person would taste the sugar and would be aware of the sweetness, but if asked to describe it, would be unable to do so. In the same way, since you are viewing your own mind, you can experience what it is like, but you could never really relate it to anyone else.

If through looking at the mind, you come to experience that the nature of the mind is what has been described—if you experience it as such through your seeing it as such when looking—then this is probably a correct experience. The only possible source of mistake here is that you might be reinforcing or adulterating your experience with conceptual understanding. For example, through study and so forth, you might have come to the conclusion intellectually that the mind must be insubstantial and therefore beyond existence, and that it must not be an absolute nothingness and must therefore by beyond non-existence. In that way, you might have an intellectual understanding that is similar to what is experienced directly. But if it's merely an intellectual understanding, then it's not a basis for liberation; it won't lead to direct experience. Because of that, while this intellectual understanding itself is a good understanding, it tends to prevent progress, because an understanding itself cannot lead to the qualities [of the awakened state] as experience can—and is therefore really no help. We can't say that having an intellectual understanding of such profound teachings is utterly useless. Of course, there is some benefit to it; there's some blessing. But it has no use whatsoever in the immediate future. It's not going to lead to anything right now. The only thing that's going to lead to anything right now is actual experience. When you look at the mind, you need to look at it without such presuppositions so that the understanding can arise on the basis of experience, internally and spontaneously. Intellectual understanding somehow has to be used to fuel experience. On the other hand, if the student has actually recognized this from within and has actually experienced lucidity-emptiness, then that is the arising or attainment of vipashyana on the basis of stillness, which is pointed out in that way. That is what is called the recognition of simultaneous arising and liberation (and all the other elegant terms that there are in all the commentaries). The student at that point has seen their mind's nature within stillness.

If you continue to practice meditation, then your experience will gradually increase and there will be greater and greater stability and greater and greater lucidity. However, the experiences that can arise in meditation can take various different forms. And in spite of the fact that the person has a real recognition of the mind's nature, there is still the possibility or probability of fluctuation in experience even after that. Sometimes you may feel that you have amazing, tremendous meditation, and at other times you may feel that you have no meditation at all. This characterizes meditation experience, which fluctuates a great deal. Realization, which is distinct from experience, does not change, but experiences can fluctuate a great deal or alternate between good and bad. There will still be times when you will have what you regard as good experiences and, in contrast, what you regard as bad experiences. When that occurs, just keep on looking. Don't get distracted or sidetracked by the experience. Whatever meditation experience arises, you should recognize that it is transitory. As is said, "meditation experience is like mist, it will surely vanish." Experiences are different from the actual fact of the recognition itself. Because they are ephemeral experiences, they aren't worth investing in. So if you have a bad meditation experience, do not be alarmed, because it too will vanish. If you have good meditation experience, you need to continue; if you have bad meditation experience, you need to continue. In either case, you simply need to continue to rest in this recognition of the mind's nature.

In themselves, experiences are good, because they indicate that there's a process occurring. The problem with experience is that you tend to fixate on it, and fixation on experience is a problem, principally because memory exaggerates. When you recollect an experience, whatever it was, you will tend to embellish it in your memory. This can happen quite quickly. Then, when you next meditate, you will be looking for the recurrence of that same experience. But even if the experience you had were to recur, because you remember it as better than it really was, you've set yourself up for disappointment. Furthermore, the whole process has become goal-oriented; you're directing your practice toward recapturing a specific experience. Obviously, conceptual contrivance has seeped in.

What's recommended is that if you have a "good experience," don't get too excited. And if you have a "bad experience," don't mistake it for a serious deviation or a sidetrack that you have to find your way back from. If you have a bad experience, just continue practicing as you were. In other words, whatever happens, just keep looking at your mind.

In *The Rain of Wisdom,* we find the story of Gampopa's receiving meditation instruction from Milarepa. Milarepa would give Gampopa instruction, he would practice, and then he would return to his teacher and describe his experiences to him. During this process, Gampopa had quite a variety of meditation experiences, including many visions. One time he saw the deity Chakrasamvara, all in white. Another time he saw the deity Chakrasamvara, all in red. Each time he went to tell Milarepa, and Milarepa would say, "Well, it's not a problem, and it's not good either. It just really doesn't mean anything. Just go back and practice." Another time, Gampopa had a clear vision of the particular hell realm that's called the "Black Line Hell." The entire valley, in which he was practicing, seemed to become completely dark, and he couldn't see much of anything. He went to Milarepa, and Milarepa just said, "Well, it's not a problem, and it's not good either. Just keep on practicing."

In this interchange, Milarepa says that worrying about meditation experiences is like worrying about what you see when you press your eyes and you see double. He says if you press your eyes and you look at the moon, you're likely to see two moons. Now, if someone were particularly naive, and they pressed their eyes and saw two moons, then they might think, "Ha! I'm really something special. Everybody else just sees one moon. I see two." Or, on the other hand, they might think, "I'm really in trouble now. Everybody sees one moon and I see two." So, when you have meditation experiences, it's like seeing two moons when you press your eyes, they're neither good nor bad. They're not problems, and they're not beneficial in themselves. Just continue.

This section in the text continues in much the same vein. What you experience when you recognize the nature of your mind within stillness is a state of stillness; in other words, the conceptuality or elaboration of thought has been at least temporarily pacified. So it is stillness. But because there's recognition of your mind's nature, it's not blank obscurity. There is also present a sort of glaring or vivid, brilliant lucidity. The recognition of the mind within stillness, if it is genuine, includes a one-pointed tranquility or shamatha, where the mind is one-pointedly engaged in the virtue of recognizing its own nature. In that, the mind is at rest comfortably and naturally. Because the recognition is nonconceptual, and because the mind is in a state of rest, what you experience is inexpressible. It's beyond any kind of apprehension, because there's no solidity to what you experience. However, you are experiencing. You can't say you're experiencing something existing or something not existing, but you are experiencing that nature, even though it's inexpressible and indescribable. What you experience is a nature that is beyond arising and cessation. Because it has no substance, it has never arisen. It's empty. But it is also beyond cessation, because it is at the same time a lucidity that is unceasing. The recognition of this nature, if it occurs within stillness, is the arising of insight or vipashyana in stillness, and is recognizing the result of the first of the five ways of looking.

This viewing of the mind within stillness needs to be practiced, not merely for one session, but many times continually. It begins with allowing your mind to come to rest in the state of shamatha. Then look at the mind in that state while continuing to rest in the mind or while looking at the mind. One thing that needs to be addressed is that the state of stillness, which is the basis for the viewing of the mind, could be one of two types of stillness. There is a type of stillness or tranquility that consists of an obscurity of mind, or mental darkness, and there is another type of stillness that consists of a non-conceptual lucidity. The state of non-conceptual lucidity is considered to be faultless stillness, and the state of mental obscurity is considered to be defective stillness. In order to engage in the vipashyana practice of looking at the mind within stillness, the stillness must be the lucid or clear kind. Essentially, this clear stillness consists of a mind that is placed in one-pointedness with the faculties of mindfulness and alertness. With the presence of mindfulness and alertness this one-pointedness of mind becomes what is called a virtuous one-pointedness, rather than a neutral or obscure one-pointedness.

Whether it is the time of your initial recognition of the mind's nature, or your subsequent cultivation of that recognition, you are viewing something that has no substantial characteristics such as shape or color, origination, cessation, and so on. You are viewing the mind's nature, which is emptiness, but which nevertheless can be experienced by you directly. When you are looking at this nature, then that which is looking at the nature and that nature which is being viewed should not be experienced as separate. If they are, then there is still some fixation on an apprehending subject and an apprehended object. In fact, such fixation is unnecessary, because that which is looking and that which is being viewed are insubstantial, are free from origination and cessation; whereas something that is substantial could be said, relatively, to have a beginning and an end. That which is insubstantial does not. Therefore, there really is no separation between that which is viewing the mind and that mind which is viewed.

It is important first to recognize this nature, and then to foster or cultivate the recognition of it. Why is this so significant? In the sutras it was said by the Buddha that the recognition of the dharmata and the subsequent attainment of Buddhahood are both far from easy. According to the sutras, in order to obtain Buddhahood, one has to gather the accumulations for three periods of innumerable *kalpas*. And in order to realize dharmata one needs to gather the accumulations through the two paths of accumulation and juncture for one of these three periods of innumerable kalpas. In short, according to the sutras, it takes a very long time and a great deal of considerable austerity in order to realize dharmata and attain awakening. But according to the oral instructions of the siddhas of our lineage, this can be done in one lifetime and in one body. In this one lifetime one can attain the state of unity, the state of Vajradhara. And this is not just a saying or a tradition. It is something that is actually possible, and it is possible because of the profundity of the instructions.

Because of the profundity of these instructions it is important to have trust and faith in them, and devotion for them. When one understands their profundity, one will meditate upon them. However, sometimes, and for some individuals, because these instructions are so profound and yet so simple and seem so easy, one's mind is unsatisfied by them. It may be difficult to trust the fact that something that is so relatively simple could actually bring one all the way to awakening. In order to accommodate this anxiety, a variety of different methods have been taught. For example, there are the practices of the Six Dharmas of Naropa, which involve many elaborate visualizations, physical exercises, and a variety of other methods, and therefore, for individuals who suspect the simplicity of mahamudra, are far more trustworthy [laughter]. In addition, there are also the many sadhanas of the creation stage connected with various yidams. And for those people who find mahamudra too simple, then these inspire greater faith and devotion and therefore are more effective. But the reason that these elaborate practices are more effective for those individuals is simply because those individuals have greater trust in them. It is not that there is anything lacking in the practice of mahamudra per se. If one has equal trust in it, then simply this mahamudra path of liberation itself is enough to complete the whole path.

Therefore, the practice of vipashyana, or lhag tong, meditation is very important. With regard to this, Jamgon Kongtrul Lodro Thaye said that, although we all seem to think that the realization of the mind's nature is very difficult and hard to understand, why should it be? It is not the case at all that it is something far away from us, for which we need to search avidly. If anything, it is too close to us, because it is right here, right in our midst. And second, it is not because it is too subtle or too profound or too difficult to understand, that we do not realize it. We do not see it because it is too easy and too simple and too obvious. It is not the case that there is anything we need to do to this mind's nature in order to realize it. Even if we were to accept that the mind's nature is within us and is right here all the time, if we think that we have to somehow alter it or improve it or get it into fit shape in order to be able to see it directly, then of course that could be difficult. But we do not have to do anything to the mind's nature. We do not have to change anything bad into anything good; we do not have to get rid of anything that exists, or create anything that does not exist. If you simply see your mind as it is, just as it is right now, that in itself will generate great meditation. This is therefore both easy and profound.

For the practice of Vajrayana in general, and especially for the meditations of mahamudra or dzogchen, it is of the utmost importance for the practitioner to have trust, faith, and devotion. In particular, with regard to devotion, which consists of enthusiasm and respect, this enthusiasm for the recognition of the nature of the mind is essential. Sometimes it is possible while one is practicing that one might come to the idea, "Well, there is nothing to see, so this is quite pointless." At such times you need to remember that while there is nothing particular to see, there is definitely something that can be experienced and realized. So this is anything but pointless. Sometimes it may happen that while you are practicing you may wonder, "Am I really just wasting my life by doing this?" It is important at those times to remember that this is not a waste of time, because by doing this practice you can actually realize the ultimate nature and attain liberation. In short, by trusting the validity of the practice and instructions, and therefore having enthusiasm and respect for the practice, your practice will go well and you will attain the result.

Sometimes when you are practicing and you are not having great experiences, it is possible that you might lose heart. It is at those times that you need especially to generate greater faith and devotion, and in order to do that, to supplicate.[32] Through supplication the blessings will definitely enter your heart, which will automatically lead to excellent meditation experience. So from time to time while you are practicing mahamudra, you should continue to supplicate both the root and lineage gurus, and sometimes augment your practice with the practices of the creation and completion stages.

The practices of mahamudra and dzogchen are distinct in the sense that the methods of the teaching and the methods of practice vary slightly, and of course, the lineages are to some extent distinct. However, they both essentially come down to the single one point of the identification of the mind's nature, which in both mahamudra and dzogchen teaching is pointed out directly, and in both cases leads to a recognition of the nature of all things. While one can make distinctions between the methods of practice in very subtle ways, essentially the practice and the teaching consist of pointing out and identifying this same one thing.

If you practice and if you are fortunate, then authentic meditation experience and recognition of the mind's nature may arise for you fairly quickly. On the other hand, although it is easy to recognize the mind's nature, because we have a long-standing or beginningless habit of not looking at it, then we can also get confused. We can be misled by our conceptual understanding, or we can be misled by various experiences, or we can simply get involved in other things that prevent us from seeing the mind's nature. In those situations, although it is better if there has been an authentic recognition, even if we have not recognized the mind's nature, to have put some effort into doing so is still very good. It was said by the Buddha that if someone goes to a place of practice and meditates, that is excellent. But if someone even takes one step towards a place of practice and for some reason gets interrupted and does not get there, there is still great benefit. There is still great merit and they are still very fortunate.

The Buddha did not say this without reason. There is a very specific reason why this is true. In order to attain the ultimate result of practice, of course we need to accomplish an extraordinary samadhi. And if we can do that, then that is excellent. But even to think that the accomplishment of such meditation is great, and that it is something necessary that we wish to do, creates a very subtle but definite habit in our minds for its cultivation. Of course, the simple wish to cultivate it does not immediately cause this meditative state and its attendant awakening to arise. Nevertheless, the inculcation of this subtle habit will cause the habit to increase and grow, and gradually one will come to have more faith, devotion, and diligence, and so on, and eventually from this seed of interest will grow this great tree of awakening. Therefore, there is a reason for the Buddha's statement that there is great merit and good fortune in even attempting to meditate. We really are fortunate in having this opportunity to practice and study mahamudra.

6 LOOKING AT THE MIND IN MOVEMENT

Previously we looked at looking at the mind within stillness, which means looking at the nature of the mind within the experience of the stability of shamatha, and also at pointing out or identifying the nature of the mind in the context of stillness.

Normally, we think that the mind exists, that our disturbing emotions exist, and that our thoughts exist. We are correct to think so, if we consider them merely as appearances. Actually, when we aren't looking directly at the mind's nature, we only experience the appearance of an existent mind, the appearance of existent thoughts and disturbing emotions. Because when we look directly at the mind to see where it is, what it is, and what its characteristics are, we discover that it has no substantial existence. This is true not only when the mind is at rest, or in a state of stillness, but also when the mind is in a state of movement and thoughts are arising. In either case, the mind is devoid of substantial characteristics such as shape and color.

As you practice the meditation of looking directly at the mind, at some point you will have a recognition of the basic nature of mind. This could happen immediately, or it could happen after some time of gradually overcoming your previous habit of not looking at the mind. In any case, that experience will be the recognition of the mind in the context of stillness, with the mind at rest. The second technique presented in the discussion on vipashyana is looking at the mind within movement or occurrence. Occurrence here refers to the arising of thought, so this technique consists of looking at the nature of thoughts as they arise. When you meditate, sometimes your mind is at rest, without any thoughts passing through it, but sometimes movement occurs. Just as it is possible to recognize the mind's nature in the context of stillness, it is equally possible to recognize it in the context of occurrence.

A distinction needs to be made between the nature of how things are, and appearances, which is how things appear. The nature of how things actually are, is experienced by an unconfused mind, and appearances, how things appear to be, is experienced by a confused mind or a confused cognition. Sometimes these are also referred to as absolute truth and relative truth, respectively. Through the confusion that generates the appearances or the projections of confusion, we come to suffer and to experience impediments and upheavals of all kinds. Because all of this suffering, these upheavals, and so forth, result from confusion, and therefore result from a mistaken view of how things are, all of these things can be removed. They are removed by coming to correctly recognize how things are or by coming to recognize the nature of all things, and it is for this reason that we devote ourselves to looking at the nature of our mind.

The reason why there are these two techniques — looking at the mind within stillness and looking at the mind within occurrence — is that, from the point of view of how things appear, stillness and occurrence are quite distinct. The one, stillness, is a state where there are no thoughts arising in the mind, and the other, occurrence, is one in which there are thoughts, possibly very coarse and disturbing thoughts, arising in the mind; but from the point of view of the nature of things, these two states are not different at all. When you look at the mind within stillness you do not find anything substantial whatsoever. And when you look at the mind within occurrence, no matter how coarse or vivid the thoughts may be, when you look at the nature of those thoughts, their nature seems to be without any substance or substantiality and to be that same emptiness that was the nature of the mind in stillness. It is in order to make this clear to us that we practice both of these as separate techniques.

The Six Consciousnesses

In general, when Buddhists classify various aspects of mind, we tend to talk either about six consciousnesses or about eight consciousnesses. If we look at the six-fold classification, these six consciousnesses are all classified as unstable consciousnesses. The first is the visual consciousness. Normally, we tend to think that it is our eyes that see things. However, because the eye itself is organic matter, and in itself cannot see, it serves as the organic support for vision. In fact, what is occurring in a moment of seeing is that the eye consciousness, which is what actually sees, is generated on the basis of the organic support of the eye contacting the objective support, which is a visually perceivable form. In other words, vision is the generation of a visual consciousness on the basis of the contact between the eye and its object.

The second consciousness is the auditory consciousness based on the organic support of the ear, and the objective basis is sounds of all types. With the organic support of the ear and the objective sounds, an auditory consciousness is generated.

The third consciousness is called the olfactory consciousness. Its organic support is the nose, and its objective basis is the various smells that we can smell. The fourth is the taste consciousness. Its organic support is the tongue, and the objective bases are the various tastes which we can experience with the support of the tongue, such as sweet, sour, salty, and bitter.

The fifth consciousness is called the body consciousness. This is the consciousness of tactile sensations, so it can also be called the tactile consciousness. Its organic support is distinct from the others. The other four sense organs — the eyes, the ears, the nose, and the tongue — are called particular sense organs, as they are in particular places within the body. The organic support for the tactile consciousness, however, is called the pervasive organ, because everywhere in the body is able to experience tactile sensations. Therefore, the organic support for this consciousness is your entire body. The objective bases are the various tactile sensations that you can experience, such as smooth, rough, hot, cold, and so on.

These five sensory consciousnesses, because they are functioning on the basis of the five sense organs, are called the consciousnesses of the five gates. A further characteristic of these five consciousnesses is that they all experience information directly. The eye consciousness sees directly, the ear consciousness hears directly, the nose consciousness smells directly, the tongue consciousness tastes directly, and the tactile consciousness feels directly. Moreover, these five sensory consciousensses are non-conceptual, which means that they can only replicate the appearance that they experience. For example, when your eye consciousness sees something, it sees what is there, but it is incapable of identifying the object or evaluating it in any sense, such as judging it as good or bad.

The sixth consciousness is the mental consciousness, and it is quite different from these first five. It has no particular organic support, but it follows the production of the first five sensory consciousnesses. So a mental consciousness can be generated on the basis of an eye consciousness of form, an ear consciousness of sound, a nose consciousness of smell, a tongue consciousness of taste, or a tactile consciousness of a tactile sensation. Following the initial sense consciousness, a mental consciousness will be generated, which develops further. It can also arise on its own, independent of any sense experience.

The object of the sixth consciousness includes forms, sounds, smells, tastes, tactile sensations, and so on. Whereas the first five consciousnesses experience their individual objects directly, the sixth consciousness does not. For example, the eye consciousness actually sees something, but the mental consciousness will generate a similitude of what the eye saw as a mental impression, which is referred to in the texts as an approximation. And the approximation is further adulterated by the process of evaluation, which is a function of the mental consciousness. For example, when your eye consciousness sees a cup, it just replicates the sense impression of what it sees. Then, when it enters the mental consciousness, a mental image, which is a vague impression of whatever the eye consciousness saw, is retained. This is combined with, and becomes a basis for, subsequent appraisal: first of all, the concept "cup," then good cup or bad cup, and then comparing it to other cups.

The eye consciousness is incapable of generating a concept, such as "cup." Therefore, it does not appraise or recognize as such. The sixth consciousness, however, is conceptual, and therefore it confuses the actual sensory experience and the name that we affix to that sense experience. It will also confuse a previous sense experience and a present one. For example, when you see a cup and generate a mental consciousness of that image, you will recognize it as the cup that you think you saw yesterday, and therefore you will have the concept of it being the same cup. All these sorts of mental manipulations are the functions of the mental consciousness.

The sixth consciousness, like the first five, is called an unstable consciousness, which means that none of these six consciousnesses are always there. They are generated through the coming together of the conditions which generate them. For example, a given sense consciousness is generated upon the contact between that sense organ and an appropriate object.

For meditation we need to examine the sixth consciousness because it is the sixth mental consciousness that performs the meditation. It is the sixth consciousness that is the subject of the meditation. To understand this, consider the technique of looking at mind within occurrence. In this technique, while you are in a state of stillness, you allow a thought to arise. The thought arises in the sixth consciousness and it is this sixth consciousness that thinks.

Looking at Occurrence

According to the commentaries, one begins the practice of looking at the mind within occurrence by cultivating a state of shamatha, as in the previous technique. You allow your mind to rest relaxed in the stillness of shamatha and then, having experienced that stillness, one of two things will happen: either a thought will arise suddenly of itself without your intentionally generating it, in which case, that thought could be any kind of thought —a thought of pleasure or of misery, a virtuous thought, a non-virtuous thought, and so on. In any case, a thought will arise, or if a thought does not arise by itself, you can intentionally generate a thought. In either case you now have a thought as the focus or support for the meditation, the nature of which thought you will look at. While the focus of this technique is different from the focus of the previous one — in that here you are looking at the nature of a thought that has arisen, whereas in the previous one you were looking at the nature of that mind which experiences stillness — the mode of meditation is exactly the same. Here, looking at the thought, you look to see where it is, where it came from, what its substance or nature is, what it is that has generated the thought, what it is or who it is that is thinking, and so forth.

When a thought arises in your mind in that way, then of course you are aware that the thought has arisen and you cannot argue with the fact that there is the appearance of a thought having arisen. A thought did arise or has arisen in your mind. The thought could have any of a vast number of forms. It could be a pleasant or an unpleasant thought, a virtuous or a non-virtuous thought, and so on. In any case, this appearance of a thought arising in your mind is a relative truth, or kundzop, it is how things appear.[33] Having recognized that the thought has arisen, then simply look directly at it. Look directly at its essence or its nature, at how things are, through looking at the thought. This does not involve searching for anything particularly difficult to find or anything particularly subtle, for that matter. And it is different from following the thought, or, allowing that thought (which could be, for example, a thought of anger toward someone you view as an enemy) to produce a further thought; it is also different from analyzing the thought by examining its content and reflecting upon the thought. From this point of view, the content of the thought is irrelevant. Whether the thought is a good thought or a bad thought really doesn't matter. In either case, it's an appropriate subject for the meditation. Don't try and figure out why you had that particular thought. Simply look directly at the thought itself, rather than at the content of the thought. And that's what's meant by looking at the nature of the thought.

You simply look directly at the thought to observe its nature. For example, does this thought that is present in your mind have a shape? Does it have a color? If it has a shape or a color, what shape or what color? As you look you will find that you do not discover a shape, you do not discover a color. Well, if it does not have a shape or color, then what substantial characteristics does it possess? If it truly exists it must possess some kind of observable characteristic. As in the previous technique, you need to look at the thought directly, which is to say that you look at the thought of the present

with the mind of the present. You do not look at the thought of the past with
the mind of the present. In other words, you look at the thought of the first
instant with the mind of the first instant, and the thought of the second
instant with the mind of the second instant. You do not look at the thought
of the first instant with the mind of the second instant, and so on. In any case,
as you look at the thought which definitely has arisen, while you are aware
that the thought is present, there is nothing that you can see or detect directly.

The Nine Questions for Looking at the Mind within Occurrence

In particular, as with the previous techniques, there are several specific ways
to look at the object, which, in the case of this technique, is the thought that
has arisen. In the way things appear, there is the appearance of a thought
arising, abiding, and ceasing. There are nine questions in this section. Again,
not all of them are, strictly speaking, questions. The first question, or part of
the technique, the first way to look at the thought, is to look at these three
aspects of the thought's presence. With regard to its arising, how does it arise?
How does the thought come into experience or come into being? From where
does it arise? Then with regard to its abiding, how does it abide? What does
it actually mean that a thought is present or is abiding, and where exactly does
it abide? And then with regard to its cessation, how does it cease? How does
the thought cease to be present and where does it go? Where does it end up
when it ceases? This is the first part of looking at thought.

The second part of the technique is working with a variety or succession
of thoughts, rather than one thought, allowing or causing a series of thoughts
to arise, and looking at their nature in sequence. This part of the technique
is especially used to work with the kleshas. You can use any of the three pre-
dominant kleshas—thoughts that are primarily characterized by ignorance,
attachment, or aggression—and you can use whatever arises; or, if necessary, you can intentionally generate a klesha. The way of looking at kleshas
here is quite distinct and particular. Normally, for example, when we want
to deal with the klesha of anger, then we distance ourselves from it, and we
look at it as though it were an object separate from ourselves, and we say,
"This anger has arisen in me, I am now angry. The object of my anger is so
and so, whom I regard as my enemy," and so forth. We distance ourselves
from the thought of anger, and also, we concern ourselves primarily with
how the thought appears, with the contents of the anger. Here, when you
look at the klesha, you look at it in a very different way. You look at it directly,
as is said in the texts, "nakedly," without anything in between you and it, so
that you look to try to find the anger itself, the very essence of this thought,

rather than merely the contents or form of the thought. You look to see exactly, where is this anger that appears to be present and what exactly is it? What substantial characteristics does it truly have? Through looking for the anger in that way, you come to see that its nature is emptiness. This does not mean that then anger vanishes; the anger is still present, but once its nature has been seen, it is without any kind of fixated apprehension. Then you can apply the same technique to other kleshas, to various thoughts of pleasure and pain, and virtuous thoughts, such as love, compassion, and so on.[34] And you will discover in the same way, that all of these thoughts have emptiness as their basic nature. The Buddha taught that all thoughts are empty, and he never said that something that was not empty was empty.

Next comes the third way of looking at thoughts. The idea of having so many different techniques is that if one does not help, then the next one will, and also, that each of them will generate a slightly different experience of looking at the nature of thought. This third technique is concerned with the distinction between the thought itself and the object of that thought — for example, a thought of pleasure or pain, or a thought of a specific klesha and the object that appears to be the basis for the arising of that specific thought. This does not mean that you investigate the thought to try and determine when that thought has arisen; it is not a question of thinking about the thought, like determining, "I am angry at so and so, because of such and such." It means to actually look in order to try to find the presence of that object in your mind. The reason for this is that when, for example, you become angry, part of becoming angry is the arising of an image of the object of your anger as a focus for that in your mind. Here, rather than looking at the anger itself, you look at the image of the object of focus and try to see where it is, this image or concept: where is it in your mind? How does it arise, and from where does it arise, and so on? Also in connection with this third technique, try to detect the difference between thoughts when their nature has been looked at, and thoughts when their nature has not been looked at.

These first three ways of looking at thought are actually distinct techniques, or distinct ways, to view the nature of thought. The next set of techniques are more descriptions of experiences you might have while looking at the thoughts. The fourth is as follows: sometimes when people look at the nature of thought, they have the experience that there is nothing whatsoever to be apprehended in a fixated way, that the thoughts have emptiness beyond elaboration as their nature. In particular, when looking for a place of origin, a place of abiding, and a place of cessation or disappearance for the thought, they find nothing whatsoever. You should regard your experience, or view your experience, to see if this is what you are experiencing. Another experience that might occur is that you become aware of the thought's arising, and then you look at the thought and, through looking at its nature, the thought disappears.

The next experience is when, from the moment of the thought's arising, there is nothing whatsoever in it to be apprehended, and in that way the thought is self-liberated—in the sense that simultaneous with its arising is its absence of substantiality, which is clearly experienced by the meditator. The distinction between the foregoing one, the fifth one, and this, the sixth one, is that in the fifth one the thought appears to be somewhat substantial as it arises, but disappears upon being looked at. In this one, from the moment of its arising it seemed to be insubstantial.

Following the sixth experience, where the thought is experienced to be insubstantial or nothing whatsoever from the moment of its inception, comes the description of the seventh. If you have had the sixth experience, then you should look at the difference between the experience of insubstantiality or emptiness in stillness, and the experience of it within thought or occurrence. You should look to see, is there any difference between what is experienced when you look at the mind within stillness, and what is experienced when you look at the mind in occurrence, when you look at the thoughts that arise. From a conceptual point of view, of course, we would say there is a difference, because these two states are distinct. In one state, stillness, no thoughts are present, in the other state, occurrence, thoughts, possibly coarse or vivid thoughts, are evident in the mind. But this is a difference in how things appear, this does not necessarily mean there is a difference in how they are. If you look at these two states and compare them, you will discover that, just as when looking at the mind within stillness, you do not discover any place of stillness in which the mind is at rest or any resting mind; then, in the same way, when you look at the mind within occurrence, you do not discover any place where this movement—this arising, dwelling, and ceasing—of thoughts is occurring. Nor do you discover any substantial thought that is arising and ceasing, and so forth.

Next described is the eighth experience, which occurs when some conceptual effort is made to apprehend the thought's arising and, as a result, you tend to label the thought, based on some concept about its nature. So you affix the labels of emptiness, cognitive lucidity, and so forth, to the thought, which is distinct from actually seeing its nature without any kind of conceptual overlay.

The ninth type of experience described is when the thought arises as though of itself, and its arising is recognized without effort and without any kind of conceptual overlay. And from the moment of its arising the thought is without any kind of effort on your part to see it in this way, and is experienced as liberated simply through having arisen — [experienced] as being in its nature the expression or embodiment of the emptiness which is its nature. You should look to see if this kind of experience arises as well.

With regard to the use of the seven questions in the previous section and the nine questions in this section, various experiences will arise for you as you practice, and there are various possibilities of what can occur. Don't misuse these questions to influence, limit, or prejudice your experience; don't corrupt your experience with your understanding. Just leave room for a direct experience of your own mind, without prejudice or influence by what you know or understand.

Sometimes when we begin to practice this type of meditation, we hope for an elegant and lucid meditative state. While it is our basic intention to look without prejudice at our mind we become disappointed with what we experience, so we try to crank it up a little bit, to fix it or improve it. Don't do that. Just look at your mind as it is. Don't feel that you have to improve it or influence it in any way. Simply rest in a direct and unprejudiced experience of your mind as it is, and don't hope for something better than whatever you actually experience.

Summary of Looking at the Mind When Thoughts Arise

These nine ways of looking at thought make up the technique of viewing the mind within occurrence. This technique, viewing the mind within occurrence, is very important because we begin our practice with shamatha. Through the practice of shamatha we develop a relationship with our thoughts that has some preference and attachment to it. Because we are attempting to cultivate a state of non-distraction, then we develop an attitude that is pleased when the mind is still, and disappointed or unhappy when thoughts arise. We become attached to stillness, and we become averse to occurrence. We often get to the point where we view thoughts as enemies or obstructors and view stillness as a friend and as a boon. There is nothing really wrong with that attitude in the context of shamatha practice, because indeed one is attempting to develop a state of tranquility; but it eventually has to be transcended, and it is transcended by this technique where you come to view the dharmata, the nature of things, which is itself ultimate peace and tranquility, within thoughts, because this is the nature of thoughts as well.

The Lineage Prayer

It is for this reason that in our Kagyu lineage supplication we recite the line, "as is taught, the nature of thoughts is the dharmakaya." This very famous quotation has become an object of disputation for certain scholars, who have said that the Kagyu view that thoughts are dharmakaya is incorrect, because thoughts are characteristic of confusion, thoughts are themselves confusion, and the dharmakaya is unconfused. Therefore, thoughts could not possibly be dharmakaya. However, as valid as their point may be, we do not say that thoughts are dharmakaya; we say that the nature of thoughts is dharmakaya, which is quite distinct. Our point is not that thoughts in themselves may not be the messengers of confusion, but that the nature of thought need not be fought, need not be viewed as threatening or as something that we need to get rid of. While thoughts, indeed, may be confusion, the nature of any thought, regardless of how confused it may appear to be, is always the unity of cognitive lucidity and emptiness, and therefore it is the dharmakaya.

In the next line of the lineage supplication it says, "nothing whatsoever, they nevertheless arise as anything, or can arise as anything." This means that there is no limit to the variety of vivid appearances which thoughts can present. Thoughts can be extremely virtuous or non-virtuous, can be very pleasant or unpleasant; thoughts can be of the nature of joy or the nature of misery, and so on. Yet no matter how vivid and how varied their appearance may be, the nature of each and every thought is nothing whatsoever, it has no substantial existence at all. In that sense, thoughts are somewhat like the wind, which blows and affects things but can never be grasped and is in a sense insubstantial. This nature of thought is discovered in direct experience and not by thinking about it. When you look at your mind directly and you look at the thoughts that arise, you discover that they have no nature in the sense of substantial characteristics. They have no place from which they proceed, no place of origin, no place of abiding, no place of cessation. They do not go anywhere when they disappear. In short, when you look for any of these things—for substantial characteristics, for an origin, location or destination of thoughts, and so on—you do not find anything whatsoever, and this not finding of any of these things is the discovery of the nature of thought.

When you look directly at thoughts you find nothing whatsoever. It is not the case that the thoughts had some kind of coarse substantiality which was destroyed by your viewing them, nor is it the case that there is a defect in the nature of thoughts which is corrected by your viewing them. From the very beginning all thoughts have always been liberated in their nature simultaneously with their arising. From the very beginning all thoughts have been empty in their nature all along. Therefore, when the Buddha taught emptiness, he taught not only the emptiness of the mind of stillness, but the emptiness of thoughts, the emptiness of the mind of occurrence. Both of these, in their nature, are equally emptiness or dharmata. Both of these are equally beyond the extremes of being something or nothing, beyond the extremes of existence and non-existence. It is not the case that by coming to recognize this or by coming to view this nature of thoughts, we change or improve the nature. It is not the case that we are creating something by seeing the nature of thoughts directly. It is simply that through seeing the nature of thoughts as they are, through recognizing thoughts to be what they are, we attain liberation, and the recognition of the nature of thoughts is sufficient for this.

Upon receiving this kind of instruction about the nature of thoughts, when you actually go on to look at the nature of thoughts directly, you may be able quite quickly to recognize the nature of thoughts and thereby resolve once and for all their nature to be emptiness. On the other hand, it is possible that you might not be able to recognize the nature of thoughts because you are still overwhelmed by the vivid content of the appearance of thoughts — vivid appearances of thoughts of aggression and passion and so on — which seem so substantial and real to you that you cannot see through them and see their nature. You should not be discouraged if you have this experience, because it is by no means an impossible or difficult task to recognize the nature of thoughts; you may simply have to keep at it for a while.

This presentation of viewing the mind within occurrence is the second of the five ways to view the mind taught in this text. Having received this instruction, please apply it in your experience. Essentially it consists of generating a state of shamatha, and then within that shamatha, allowing a thought to arise and then looking directly at that thought. This technique is of immeasurable importance because it is the actual remedy to all the confusion of thoughts and kleshas.

Questions

Question: Sometimes it seems that thoughts arise out of physical sensations. But sometimes physical sensations seem to come out of thoughts. How does that happen?

Thrangu Rinpoche: It's quite possible that a thought arising within the mental consciousness can generate physical sensations. What is occurring is that an extremely intense thought process or emotional state within the mental consciousness affects the channels and winds within the body, which then—in the case of an unpleasant sensation—are agitated, and then you feel ill.

Question: When I try to settle the mind to look at thoughts, suddenly it seems that underneath there are the emotions. I'm trying to see the thoughts, to see if there's anything there, and the emotions seem to be there underneath. Then I can't get underneath them. Is that how it is?

Rinpoche: It is very much like that. What happens when a coarse thought arises is that a lot of stuff comes along with it. In the Abhidharma, the distinction that's made about this is between the main mind and the surrounding mental arisings. What happens is that, when a concept or a thought arises (for example, a virtuous one), then it will bring a lot of virtuous mental arisings with it. And the same is true with a negative thought. There will seem to be other things surrounding or underlying the thought.

Question: I understand that the sixth consciousness, the mind, is what conceptualizes and makes judgments. In the practice of mahamudra, is that set aside? And if so, what replaces it?

Rinpoche: Generally speaking, the sixth consciousness is conceptual, and as such is considered to be confused. When one recognizes the nature of mind, then within that recognition the mind relaxes. At the same time, the thoughts, which are the expressions of the confusion become pacified and subside. Although it is true that the sixth consciousness normally is conceptual, when it is employed correctly in looking at the mind's nature, then it is in a non-conceptual state. And then the mode of cognition of the sixth consciousness is not considered to be confused, but to be direct valid cognition. Among the four types of direct valid cognition, this is what is called yogic direct valid cognition. Thus, in that state of the mind experiencing its own nature directly, there is no conceptual confusion; that conceptual confusion has subsided.

Question: Rinpoche, earlier I heard you mention *kundzop* several times, and I wanted to ask what is the relationship between kundzop and the sixth consciousness and inferential valid cognition.

Rinpoche: First of all, I was using kundzop, which was being translated as "relative truth," and dondam, which was being translated as "absolute truth." We can say that kundzop and dondam are the two truths; and, in the context of the discussion of the sixth consciousness, then we would say that confusion is kundzop, or relative truth, and that the true nature of mind, that which is recognized in the midst of confusion, is dondam, or absolute truth. A common image given for this is mistaking a spotted rope for a snake. The imputed snake, which in fact does not exist at all, is a metaphor for kundzop; and the rope, which is what's really there, is a metaphor for dondam. Often, kundzop and dondam are explained as appearance and the emptiness of that appearance. So, in the context of meditation experience, the occurrence of thought is kundzop, or relative truth, and the emptiness that is the nature of that occurrence of thought, which is seen when it's directly looked at, is dondam, or absolute truth.

As for there being a connection between relative truth and inferential valid cognition, I cannot say yes and I cannot say no. Inferential valid cognition is the Buddhist technical term for what we would normally call logic or logical reasoning. Sometimes it is applied to the examination of relative truth, and sometimes it is applied to absolute truth. So it is not necessarily applied to relative truth. However, in the meditation experience which is the direct experience of absolute truth, since it is a direct experience, there is no inference, and therefore no inferential valid cognition involved. Instead, there is direct valid cognition. Perhaps that is what you were getting at.

The relationship between the sixth consciousness and inferential valid cognition is that when inferential reasoning is done, it is performed by the sixth consciousness. However, because the sixth consciousness is conceptual, one cannot assume that all of its conceptuality is inference, because in fact its conceptuality is fundamentally invalid; it is not a valid cognition of any kind, inferential or direct. Most of the actions by the sixth consciousness are conceptual imputations, which are not valid cognitions of any kind, based upon the direct valid cognition of the five consciousnesses and subsequent mental arisings. Sometimes the sixth consciousness can experience relative truth and can generate inferential valid cognitions, but a lot of the time, it's simply confused.

Question: Rinpoche, about the meditation instructions, I gather that this is meant to be a kind of sequentially developed process, first seeing the mind in stillness and then generating thoughts. I was wondering about actually doing that. Is this something that we just would do, get into a state of shamatha, then look at thought over and over during that period of time? And how do we decide when to move from one technique to the next?

Rinpoche: Well, the traditional way of doing it is to allot a set amount of time

✳   for each of the techniques which will be presented, such as one week on each. It could be longer than that; there's nothing wrong with that. But there's also nothing wrong with combining them and using them as appropriate. For example, when meditating, if you find that you have lots of thoughts popping up, then you could apply the second technique [looking at mind within occurrence] and if, when meditating, if you find that your mind is naturally at rest, it would be appropriate to apply the first technique [looking at mind within stillness].

Question: You said earlier that there is the mahamudra experience of awareness being aware of itself, or awareness being aware of its own awareness. And you said, "Why have we not seen this? It's because we've been under the sway of ignorance for so long." Now, is it that we actually have not experienced this, we have not seen this awareness that's aware of its own awareness, or is it we have not recognized it?

Rinpoche: Mainly, the way it's explained and understood is that we've never had the opportunity to look. We've never had the circumstances under which we could have looked. The reason is that, as we saw earlier, the mind's main qualities are intense lucidity and emptiness or insubstantiality. Now, the lucidity of mind is so intense that we are overwhelmed by it or we could say it overwhelms itself, and being overwhelmed by its own intensity, it looks outward. Now, what this means is that, if we bother to look, we will probably see or experience the mind directly. So if we look, we'll see it.

Question: Rinpoche, a couple of difficulties that I'd like to ask you about; one is the feeling that the arising of thoughts does come from somewhere. I think from my point of view it is easier to see that they're not abiding and not going anywhere, but there is a feeling that they are coming from somewhere like the storehouse consciousness.[35] The second difficulty is this business of trying to look at thoughts within that instant and not with subsequent thoughts, and this seems to me a very difficult matter, and I feel that I need some additional guidance on this.

Rinpoche: To answer your first question first: The understanding, for example, that the source of thoughts is the habits placed in the all-basis consciousness is a valid understanding. But it is an understanding within the context of relative truth about how things appear; that is, in the context of relative truth, it is a way of understanding the appearance of thoughts. Here we are concerned with absolute truth, which is not an object of understanding of the intellect at all and can only be experienced or appreciated through looking directly at something—in this case, looking directly at thoughts. For example, if you were meditating and you were looking for the origin of thoughts, and the thought arose, "Well these thoughts are coming from the all-basis consciousness," then you would look to see where the all-basis consciousness was and where it came from; and, if you keep on looking directly, not with theory but directly, you will find nothing anywhere. It is not that you are not finding anything because you do not understand what to look for, nor is it the case that you are not finding anything because you do not know how to look. You are not finding anything because there is not anything to be found. That is the nature of things and the nature of thought as opposed to the appearance of things or the appearance of thought.

With regard to your second question, as you say, when you start to work with this technique, you find that through looking at a thought that you are looking at a thought that has already vanished, and so you are looking at a thought of the past. But if you keep on going, then what will happen is that you will start to catch thoughts, or detect the arising of thoughts, and be able to actually look at the nature of thoughts as they arise, not only once they are already present and before they have vanished, but even as they are arising.

Question: Rinpoche, I have three questions. The first is a vocabulary question. Is what Rinpoche was referring to in the sixth point what is called in Tibetan, *zangtal*, or *zangtal che*? Is it the same experience? The second question is: Can Rinpoche say something more about the relationship between the sixth point and the ninth point, and what the distinction between the two is? The third one is: Would Rinpoche say something about the relationship between these nine questions or techniques and another way of looking at mahamudra, which is the progression of seeing phenomenon as mind, mind as emptiness, emptiness as spontaneous presence, and spontaneous presence as self-liberation?

Translator: The first question: Is the experience explained in the sixth point the same as what is called the experience of zangtal, which means, both penetrating and transparent or unobstructed?

Rinpoche: Yes, it is the same experience. And to reiterate the meaning of the sixth and ninth point: really, the type of experience or understanding described in the sixth and the ninth parts of the technique is the same. The difference is the context. The sixth is describing something you might experience, and the ninth is describing the same thing again as a kind of summary, concluding the technique, encouraging you to go on in that way. Essentially the sequence described here and the fourfold sequence of introduction or pointing out described in *The Ocean of Definitive Meaning* and other places — where appearances are pointed out to be mind; mind is pointed out to be emptiness; emptiness is pointed out to be spontaneous presence; and spontaneous presence is pointed out to be self-liberation — are basically the same.

Questioner: Would Rinpoche say something about hlundrup, or spontaneous presence, and particularly with respect to this technique of understanding?

Rinpoche: In this context the idea of emptiness being spontaneous presence is that, while the nature of everything is emptiness, nevertheless, that nature expresses itself or appears spontaneously, which is to say, that the appearances of things that are emptiness is not something contrived but something spontaneous or natural. Spontaneous presence being self-liberation is the idea that, because these appearances are the spontaneous display of emptiness, they are in their nature free of any kind of substantiality that requires any kind of change or improvement and, therefore, are in their nature self-liberated.

Question: Rinpoche, if I remember correctly, you talked about the mind operating in a series of small instants, little moments, and to me, having a little experience with stillness and some experience of thought, they all seem to have duration, and I guess I am not very familiar with these instants. I am wondering if this is an important thing to understand and know how they operate. It seems as if it must have some bearing on what you are discussing now, but I wonder if you might elaborate on that, please?

Rinpoche: The idea that the mind is made up of a series of moments is based on the idea that all things that are composites can be traced as a series of moments, and they are characterized as such because these things are constantly changing, at least a little bit, in every moment. Therefore, one cannot say that the thing is the same for any duration of time. This is the idea that everything, including the mind, is made up of things that are constantly changing. However, while this would include thought — since a thought, even while it appears to have duration, is undergoing some kind of change — this is all about how things appear; this is a characteristic of appearances, this instantaneity, not a characteristic of the nature of appearances. When you look at your mind directly in meditation, then you sense through the appearance of origination, the appearance of location, and the appearance of desti-nation. By seeing through the appearance of the origination or arising of thought, then you have seen through the illusion of substantiality, and, there-fore, since the thought has no substantiality to persist, it is not a persistent series of instants or moments in its nature. This is true both of the mind in stillness and the mind in occurrence. The mind in stillness is manifestly with-out any kind of substantiality; therefore, in its nature there is no change occurring, and therefore, in its nature there is no succession of moments. The mind in occurrence, however, is also that way, because, when you see directly the nature of thoughts, then you see that as the thought arises it is already liberated in its nature, because it is already free of substantiality, and therefore is free of being what it might otherwise appear to be to a deluded consciousness, which is a succession of moments.

Question: Rinpoche, I have a little bit of confusion about reconciling the mahamudra system of instruction, in which it seems basically to be saying that, because the mind's nature is naturally insubstantial and empty, it can be looked at and recognized at any time. I want to reconcile this with the com-mon presentation of the paths and levels. We are told in a very matter-of-fact way that it is utterly impossible for beginners on either the path of accumu-lation or the path of juncture to generate direct realization of emptiness, or absolute truth. What we can do at best is generate a similitude, or some-thing that is concordant with absolute truth, but we are taught that it is not the absolute truth itself. What I am wondering is, if this is the case—say if most people are at one of the first two levels of the path of accumulation, the lesser level, or the medium level—if one had the appropriate training and cir-cumstances, such as having these instructions, such as having a great deal of faith and devotion, having a lama endowed with realization, would it be pos-sible for them, given those circumstances, to suddenly generate the realiza-tion and somehow jump over these first two paths to the path of seeing? I cannot fit these two systems together in my mind.

Rinpoche: The reason, first of all, for the difference in presentation between the mahamudra systems and the sutra systems[36] with regard to the question at what point the nature of things can be directly experienced is that, in the sutra system, the practice leading to the realization of emptiness consists of the use of analysis and the use of reasoning, and there is no presentation in the sutra system of the direct pointing out of one's mind. If one uses the techniques of the sutra system alone, then one's resources consist of the gath-ering of the accumulations and the cultivation of an abstraction of emptiness, and being limited to that, then one will not have a direct realization of emptiness until the path of seeing. On the other hand, in the traditions of the Vajrayana in general, and the mahamudra in particular, the emphasis is on the direct pointing out to the student of the nature of his or her mind, and since the mind is something that is easily realized directly to be empty, then through that, one comes to have a glimpse of emptiness. Having a glimpse of the emptiness of mind, one has a glimpse of the emptiness of all things, and since emptiness of mind is the same emptiness as that of all things, in that way then, a beginner does see the dharmata, does have a glimpse of dharmata long before the path of seeing. However, at the same time, what this beginner has is a glimpse, not a continuous and stable realization of dharmata. Although, through the practice of the mahamudra system, one can gradually stabilize it and deepen it until one attains the authentic path of seeing, as far as the relationship between the wisdom that is generated by the beginner who receives the pointing out instruction and identifies the mind's nature and the wisdom of the path of seeing, we would have to say that what that beginner generates in the mahamudra system is a glimpse of the path of seeing, but is not the full and authentic attainment of the path of seeing.

Question: Rinpoche, my question is in regard to the fifth point, being aware of thoughts' arising. When you become aware of them, they seem to disappear in post-meditation experience. I am very much a beginner, but since I've been meditating, the extreme thoughts of impermanence, passion, and anger, in particular, arise, and when these thoughts arise, I've been able to catch them before they manifest. But I've hit a weird plateau in the sense that when these things arise, when I become aware of them, I tend to laugh. I find it very funny when these things happen and basically, I think it is funny that my mind is manifesting in extreme ways. I find that very humorous and then I get stuck in that, so then that moment is gone, and then I am stuck in the humor of my mind getting caught up in impermanence. Does Rinpoche have tips on how to proceed, disregard this, etc.?

Rinpoche: The answer to this is really the same as the answer to the earlier question. Through the humor and the laughter that specific thought may have disappeared, but another thought is arising, so you just wait for the next thought. You look at whatever thought is present at the time.

Same questioner: But if I keep laughing—because of being caught up in these extreme thoughts of impermanence or the extreme passion—that does continue and it sort of develops because that one thought is gone. But then I just seem to get stuck in stuff.

Rinpoche: Look at the nature of this thought of its being funny, this sensation of its being funny, and then that will dissolve. Look at the nature of whatever thought is present. It does not matter which thought you look at. As long as there is a thought present you have an opportunity to look at the nature of thought. And the nature of any of them is the same, and it is that same nature that you are trying to see.

Question: Rinpoche, I found it rather unusual that sometimes, when looking at the nature of thought as an observer, the thought disappears at that moment. Is it just an appearance and does the act of observation cause its insubstantiality?

Rinpoche: This happens when the conceptual content of the effort of looking replaces the previous thought, and so it is an appearance that is produced by your looking. The way that you look at the thought drives that thought out because it is replaced with something else. The remedy for this is the second of the nine techniques, where, rather than attempting to look at one thought, you allow a whole series of thoughts to continue, giving yourself an opportunity to actually see, not only thoughts toward the end of their duration, but to see thoughts actually coming into presence.

Question: The emptiness that is realized in stillness of the mind and the emptiness looking at the nature of one thought and the emptiness that is realized by looking at the occurrence of thought, both its origination, its abiding, and its cessation, and also the emptiness of the observer looking, are these all the same emptiness? Are they all one taste? Are there graduations of emptiness?

Rinpoche: The looking at the origin, the location, and the destination of thoughts, in particular, is more of a method designed to allow you to identify the nature of thought. But the nature of the mind in stillness and the nature of the thoughts that arise in the mind in occurrence are the same. That is, the same nature.

Question: Rinpoche, in my meditation I've had some experience with looking at thoughts in stillness and occurrence and not seeing any substance. However, it seems that I experience something that is hard to explain. It is not really a feeling even, or a thought. It seems to be something almost intangible like an irritation, or something heavy that almost seems to abide. It does seem to just stay there. I continue to look and I do not know if I just need to look more, but it seems very much present all the time.

Rinpoche: It is probably that you are just not yet used to looking in this way, and as you become more used to doing it, then this sense of irritation or discomfort or the heavy, abiding presence will be seen through.

Question: This is a question related to several that have just arisen. I am wondering about the effort that one makes in staying with the first moment and not rushing on to the second. In my own experience I find that the most difficult aspect of the meditation. I try too hard to create very quickly the second thought. What's happening? I bring myself off of that moment, it seems, through genuine effort, but how do you realize the nature of emptiness in the effort itself?

Rinpoche: First, all the effort that you describe is necessary because what you are talking about is the placement of mindfulness and alertness, but if you find that the effort itself somehow becomes a cause of distraction or disturbance, then you should look right at the nature of that distraction that occurs, or look at the nature of the effort.

7 THE NATURE OF MIND
IN MOVEMENT

I HAVE EXPLAINED the second technique of viewing the mind, which is
viewing the mind in the midst of movement or occurrence. There is now
the corresponding introduction or pointing out that goes with that way of
viewing the mind, which is pointing out the mind's nature within occurrence. The idea here is that, having practiced viewing your mind within
occurrence, you will have had some experience of this. What the experience
was might vary. You might have had an authentic recognition of the mind's
nature, or you might have had a different kind of experience. In any case, it
is the accumulation of experience itself that is important and that is dealt with
here in the introduction or pointing out. The introduction serves to help
the student understand their experience and determine whether or not it is
actually an authentic recognition of the mind's nature, and as it is set out in
Pointing Out the Dharmakaya, it consists of a dialogue between the teacher
and the student. However, having received this as instruction, you can also
use it in your individual practice to test the validity of your own experience.

First you practice looking at your mind within occurrence, and then you
try to assess the experience you have on the basis of doing so. In this text,
there are set forth essentially three different types or levels of experience one
might have. In one case one really has no experience whatsoever; in the second case one has some experience, which is to say, a partial recognition, and
in the third case there is a full experience, a full recognition. This can be discovered either through the questioning of the student by the teacher, or by
the student's questioning himself or herself.

In the first case, when asked to explain their experience, the student is
likely to say something like the following: "Well, I experienced that my mind
is empty or that my mind is emptiness or that it lacks all substantiality." If
you say that, that then is an indication that you have had no experience,
because this is a concept and jargon that you were using because you are still
trying to control your meditation through the presuppositions of theory and
dogma. Because you had that thought about the mind and you had come to

the conclusion that, well, probably the mind must be empty, it must be insubstantial—through reasoning—then this is what you say. But it is not something you discovered in meditation.

The second type of situation is when asked about their experience the student says, well what happens is that I look at a thought and at first the thought is there, but as I look at it, it dissolves and disappears and there is nothing there whatsoever. In this situation the student has some degree of experience, a partial recognition.

The third situation is one where the student has had a real or decisive experience of their mind's nature and in that case they are likely to say that they have not found anything that could be called a something or a nothing. There does not seem to be anything that could be called a something or a nothing. There does not seem to be anything that they can apprehend, and yet they feel no fixation on this absence of anything to apprehend. There is not even a separate thinker or watcher that is failing to apprehend anything in the mind. Often such a student will say that they have had the experience of seeing thoughts vanishing as they are arising, which is an indication that they have experienced a simultaneous arising and liberation of thought. In such a case, the student is instructed to continue to practice as they have been, and further practice at that point is indeed very important.

The nature of stillness and of the mind that is in a state of stillness is free from origination, abiding, and cessation. This is something that appears directly to you in your experience when you look at the mind within stillness. But whereas, before one began to practice meditation, one may have regarded the state of the occurrence of thought as fundamentally different from still- ness, since when thoughts arise, they agitate you, and so forth, once you have practiced this meditation, then you will discover that there is no real differ- ence between the nature of the mind in stillness and the nature of the mind in occurrence. Just as the nature of the mind in stillness is free from origin, location, and destination, in the same way the nature of the thoughts that arise in the context of occurrence are a union or a unity of cognitive lucid- ity and emptiness. That state of stillness itself is also such a unity of cogni- tive lucidity and emptiness. This means that not only is the nature of the mind experienced within stillness empty, but even the thoughts that are expe- rienced in occurrence have the same nature as that nature of the mind. This means that when thoughts appear to move or to occur, it does not mean that there is any substantial thing or truly existent thing that is rushing about in your mind. The thoughts themselves have the same nature as the mind that generates them. Once this has been recognized then there will no longer be any preference for stillness over occurrence, and the absence of a preference for absence over occurrence comes about because of the direct or naked seeing of both states as mere cognitive lucidities without any substantial existence.

Although one recognizes the cognitive lucidity or the lucidity of awareness within emptiness, there are different ways that this might be recognized. For example, someone might find that when they look at the nature of a thought, initially the thought arises, and then as the thought dissolves, what it leaves in its wake or what it leaves behind it is an experience or recognition of the unity of cognitive lucidity and emptiness. Because this person has recognized this cognitive lucidity and emptiness, there is some degree of recognition, but because this can only occur for them or has only occurred for them after the thought has subsided or vanished, then they are still not really seeing the nature of thought itself. For someone else, they might experience that from the moment of the thought's arising, and for the entire presence of that thought, it remains a unity of cognitive lucidity and emptiness. This is a correct identification, because whenever there is a thought present in the mind, or when there is no thought present in the mind, and whether or not that thought is being viewed in this way or not, the nature of the mind and the nature of thought is always a unity of cognitive lucidity and emptiness. It is not the case that thoughts only become that as they vanish.

The word naked is used a great deal at this point in the text. And the word naked here has a very specific and important meaning because it is used to distinguish between understanding and experience, that is to say, understanding and recognition. It is very easy to confuse one's understanding for an experience or a recognition. One might understand something about the mind and therefore think that one had recognized it directly. Here, the use of the term "naked" means "direct;" that is to say, something that is experienced nakedly or directly in the sense that the experience is free from the overlay of concepts.

Whereas normally we have the attitude that thought is something we must get rid of, in this case it is made clear that it is important not to get rid of thought, but to recognize its nature, and indeed, not only the nature of thought but the nature of stillness must be recognized. In particular, with regard to thought, as long as we do not recognize its nature, of course thought poses a threat to meditation and becomes an impediment. But once the nature of thought has been correctly recognized, thought itself becomes the meditative state and therefore it is often said that "the root of meditation is recognizing the nature of thought."

There lived in the eighteenth century a great Gelug teacher named Changkya Rolpe Dorje, who from his early youth displayed the signs of being an extraordinary person. He became particularly learned and also very realized, and at one point he composed a song called *Recognizing the Mother*. In his song, "mother" is the word he uses to refer to dharmata or the nature of one's mind. This song was so extraordinary that a commentary was written about it by Khenchen Mipam Rinpoche. In this song, Changkya Rolpe Dorje makes a very clear distinction between recognizing and not recognizing the nature of one's mind. In one part of the song he says, "Nowadays we scholars of the Gelug tradition, in discarding these appearances of the mind as the basis for the realization of emptiness and of the basis for the negation of true existence, and in searching for something beyond this to refute, something beyond this to negate in order to realize emptiness, have left our old mother behind; in other words, we have missed the point of emptiness."

Changkya Rolpe Dorje gives another image for this mistake that we tend to make. He says that we are like a small child who is sitting in his mother's lap. In the song, the mother is dharmata, the nature of things, the nature of the mind, and the child is oneself—in his song, himself. And in the song he says, I am like a child who, in his mother's lap, is held by the mother facing away from the mother and forgetting where he is, looks for his mother everywhere; looks above, below, left and right and is unable to see his mother and becomes quite agitated thinking, "Where is my mother? I've lost my mother. I can't find her anywhere." Along comes the child's older brother who reminds the child by saying, "Your mother is right here, you are in her lap." In the same way, although the nature of our mind or emptiness is with us all the time, we tend to look for it indirectly; we look for it somewhere outside ourselves, somewhere far away. And yet we do not need to look far away if we simply view the nature of thought as it is. In the song, Rolpe Dorje is discussing or praising the importance of understanding interdependence and the image the older brother represents is both the understanding of interdependence and the recognition of the nature of thought. So the metaphor for interdependence is the child's brother, who, standing in front of the child, says, "Your mother's right behind you; in fact, you're in her lap right now."

Up to now, for us, thought and the nature of thought have been hidden by thought itself, simply because we have not known how to view thought. But now, knowing how to look at or how to view thought, we are in a position superior to that in which we meditate without thought, because, far from becoming an impediment, thought becomes an opportunity for recognition. Therefore, when thoughts arise, do not fight them, just recognize them. However, recognition of thought does not simply mean being aware that a thought has arisen, or being aware of the contents of that thought. It does not simply mean, "Oh, this is a thought of anger, this is a thought of desire, this is a thought of devotion." Recognition of thought means seeing the empty essence of all of these thoughts. When you can see the essence or the essential nature of thoughts, then the arising of thought no longer means bad meditation, and the absence of thoughts no longer means good meditation, because the nature of mind never changes.

Self-Awareness

If you have studied a great deal, and in particular have studied the *Madhyamakavatara* by Chandrakirti and the *Bodhicharyavatara* by Shantideva, such as the ninth chapter in [the latter] text on prajna, then you will have encountered the statement that it is impossible for the mind to be aware of itself. This is taught in the Madhyamaka system in these texts, and many reasons are given for this statement. This would cause someone who has studied a great deal, or who was learned in the doctrine, to wonder, because in the context of mahamudra, we say that the mind *is* aware of itself. Then again, if you have studied valid cognition, and, in particular, the explanation of valid cognition composed by Dharmakirti, you will have found the statement that there *is* such a thing as self-awareness of the mind, because it is one of the four types of direct valid cognition that are taught in the study of valid cognition. If you operate under the assumption that the self-awareness spoken of in mahamudra, the self-awareness spoken of in valid cognition, and the self-awareness refuted in Madhyamaka are all the same, then you will definitely perceive a contradiction. However, the term self-awareness is used differently in each of these three contexts.

First of all, in the Madhyamaka context the self-awareness that is refuted is the mind being aware of itself as a substantial thing, that is to say, the mind as an appearance having true existence and being able to directly experience or be aware of its own truly existent characteristics. From among the two categories of things, cognitions and inert matter, mind of course is cognition, and as a cognition it is aware. What is refuted in the Madhyamaka context is that that cognition has a true or absolute existence and could, therefore, be aware of its own substantial or absolute existence. The mind is empty of substantial existence and is therefore not aware of any substantial existence within itself. In short, the mind does not see itself, or is not aware of itself, in the sense of seeing a thing.

In the mahamudra context, when we say that the mind can be aware of its own nature, we mean that the mind is aware of its own nature, which is emptiness. Of course, all things are empty, but among all things, mind is manifestly empty. When you look at your mind in the mahamudra practice you observe that there is no shape, no color, no substantial characteristic of any kind, that the mind has no true origination, abiding, or cessation. If the mind had substantial existence, it would possess these characteristics, it would come into being, it would abide, and it would cease. What the mind sees when the mind looks at its own nature is its own absence of true existence. What is refuted in the Middle Way school is the mind seeing its own presence of true existence, since it does not have any. Therefore, in the mahamudra context, the use of self-awareness is quite different from the way it is used in the Madhyamaka context.

On the other hand, in the context of valid cognition we find the statement that all mind is self-aware, which seems to be a complete contradiction of the Madhyamaka refutation of self-awareness. However, in the context of valid cognition, self-awareness has yet a third meaning. It means that you are aware of your own experience, that which is experienced by your mind is not hidden from you, is obvious to you. Therefore, if your mind was not self-aware in that way, then you would have no way of knowing what you were thinking. You would have no way of knowing what you were seeing, what you were hearing, what you were smelling, and so forth. In short, the capacity for all the experiences of the five sense consciousnesses and the sixth, the mental consciousness, is based upon self-awareness. However, this awareness of your own experience, which is called self-awareness in the context of valid cognition, is not an awareness that has a separate subject and object. On the other hand, it is still a relative truth form of self-awareness, and therefore it is different from the self-awareness spoken of in mahamudra, because the self-awareness in mahamudra is aware of absolute truth.

Thus in the mahamudra context, when we say that the mind can see itself, this is not at all like an eye seeing itself. Rather, the mind, being awareness, can experience its own awareness. In fact, this is not difficult to do at all because the mind is not looking for something far away. It's right here.

You might ask then, if it's right here, and it's always been right here, why have you never seen it? The reason is that, throughout beginningless time, we have been afflicted by ignorance and, under the sway of ignorance, we have never looked. If you look, then you can recognize the mind's true nature, which is that it has no substantial existence whatsoever and yet is not a mere nothingness or static emptiness. It is pure awareness. This is something that you can experience directly in meditation.

Now I have explained viewing the mind within occurrence and the corresponding introduction to the mind's nature within occurrence. The function, again, of the introduction or pointing out was to enable you to assess the experience you have while viewing the mind within occurrence.

If I were to say to you that through my great compassion and my wonderful blessing I will cause you to have experience and realization, or if I were to say to you that through my great compassion and blessings I will save you from samsara, I would be lying. I do not possess any compassion or any blessing, but on the other hand, I know full well that I have no intention to mislead you or fool you or guide you incorrectly. My intention in teaching is simply to provide you with that which is most beneficial. Furthermore, these teachings are not something that I have come up with myself. These are the teachings of all the Indian and Tibetan siddhas of our lineage, and it is in reliance upon these teachings and these practices that they attained supreme siddhi. Therefore I am completely confident that what I am explaining to you in this context is in no way deceptive or misleading and is completely authentic and worthwhile. Therefore, please practice it as much as you can.

8 LOOKING AT THE MIND WITHIN APPEARANCES

I N THIS TEXT of instruction on mahamudra, *Pointing Out the Dharmakaya*, the vipashyana presentation consists of five ways to view the mind or look at the mind and five corresponding introductions to the mind's nature. Of these five pairs of sections, the most important are viewing the mind within stillness and viewing the mind within occurrence. These are the most important because, in the case of viewing the mind within stillness, this teaches one how to generate the wisdom of vipashyana in the midst of the experience of the stillness of shamatha, and in the case of viewing the mind within occurrence, it teaches on how to generate this wisdom when thoughts arise within that experience of shamatha. Therefore, these two are the most important to practice and, in a sense, the most useful and beneficial.

Looking at Appearances

Now we come to the third way to look at the mind, which is looking at the mind within appearances. Generally speaking, when we present mahamudra, the format is the threefold presentation of view, meditation, and conduct.[37] From among these three topics, what we are concerned with here is view, which is very important, because it is the ground or basis of practice. There are two types of view. One is the view that comes from learning, contemplation, and study. This view is gained by thinking about the nature of things and attempting to come to an approximate understanding of it through analysis. This type of view is very hard to apply in meditation practice. The other type of view, which is characteristic of the Vajrayana, is not a conceptual position that is arrived at through analysis. View in Vajrayana is called the view of direct experience, because it is the view that is generated through the prajna of meditation that, arising as meditation experience, is able to recognize directly the [true] nature. In other texts, we find the terms, "co-emergent mind in itself," "co-emergent thought," and "the co-emergence of appearances." In this text, these same topics are presented as "looking at the mind within stillness," "looking at the mind within occurrence or thought," and now the third topic, "looking at the mind within appearances."

Two Kinds of Appearances

Now appearance refers to two aspects of experience; one is what are called external [or outer] appearances, which are externally apparent objects, and the other is what are called internal appearances, which means what appears within or what is experienced within your mind. The first of these two categories, external appearances, consists of the objects of the five senses: the forms that are perceived by the eye; the sounds that are perceived by the ear; the tastes that are perceived by the tongue; the smells that are perceived by the nose; and the tactile sensations that are perceived by the whole body. Because we have five sense organs, then we generate five sense consciousnesses which contact their respective objects, of which we then become aware. And our sense experiences are an unlimited variety of things. Forms, shapes, colors, sounds, smells, and tastes can be pleasant, unpleasant, neutral and so forth. In any case these are what is meant by the term, external appearances.

The second type of appearance we experience is inner or internal appearances which consist of, to begin with, the replication by the mind of the similitudes of what is experienced by the senses. Internal appearances include the mental images of forms, sounds, smells, tastes, and tactile sensations, and also all of the concepts generated on the basis of these, which generally start out as being [in each case] an abstraction based upon the initial sense impression. Internal appearances also include sicknesses, experiences of pain and suffering, of pleasure, of heat and cold, of joy and depression, and so on, negative states of mind such as kleshas, positive states of mind such as love and compassion, and so forth. All of these different mental experiences are called internal appearances.

Whether one is working with external, physical appearances or internal, mental appearances, in either case, the technique here is to look at the nature of these. It is somewhat harder to look at the nature of external, physical appearances, simply because we have such a deeply entrenched habit of seeing them as separate from our minds. We think of the various things we perceive (columns, vases, walls, and so on) as being external to ourselves. But what you are actually experiencing—what you are actually seeing, for example—is not out there. The appearance, that is to say, the experience of the appearance, occurs within your mind. When you see a column, a pillar, you see it within your mind. Ordinarily we think of the column as external, as being made of whatever it is made out of (plaster or cement or whatever), but in fact, what you are seeing is actually made out of the stuff of your mind. It is inseparable from your mind. Seeing, hearing, smelling, and tasting are really mental experiences. If you analyze this with reasoning, you can determine that the externally apprehended objects are not separate from the internal apprehending cognition, and you can determine through reasoning that the perceived appearances, therefore, are not composed of particles, but in fact, are mental creations or designations based on physical perception. However, we nevertheless have a very strongly entrenched habit of seeing external things as separate from ourselves, because we naturally experience our perspective or viewpoint as being a mind that is looking out at the world that is somehow outside of and separate from that perceiving mind.

What we are doing in this style or approach to looking at the mind, is using the context of the mind experiencing such an appearance to see the mind's nature within that context.

Working with External Appearances

This technique begins with looking at an object of visual perception, such as a pillar, a vase, a wall, a mountain, and so on. It could be almost anything. It could be big, it could be small, it doesn't matter. Simply direct your gaze to that chosen object of visual perception and look at it directly.

It may be helpful, in order to work with this problem, when you are meditating on external appearances in particular, to allow the focus of your eyes, the physical focus of your organ of vision, to relax. Without allowing your eyes to focus on any one thing or another, allow your vision to relax to the point where you do not see any given thing particularly clearly. This will cause a slight reduction of the vividness or intensity of visual appearances and can help generate an experience of the non-duality of appearances and mind. The particular point here is to look in a way that is relaxed so that your vision is somewhat diffused and not focused on any one thing. By allowing your vision to be unfocused you will not see the details of the forms that are present in your line of vision. The reason why this is helpful is that it is by seeing details, through focusing on a specific thing physically, that we promote or sustain our fixation on the apparent separateness of visual perception.

At this point, we need to make a distinction between this use of an object of visual perception and the use of an object of visual perception in the shamatha techniques that I explained earlier. In the techniques of shamatha or tranquility meditation, you direct your mind to a bare visual perception, for example, of a pebble or a small piece of wood. In that case, what you are doing is actually concentrating your mind on that visual perception; you try to hold your mind to that object. Here we're using the visual form in a different way. We're trying to use the experience of visual perception as an opportunity to discover or reveal the mind's nature, to see the emptiness or insubstantiality that is inseparable from the vividness of the perceptual experience. So what we are really looking at here is not the object but the nature or essence of the experience of the object, which is the unity of emptiness and lucidity.

In this technique, look with your eyes in a way that is very relaxed so that, not seeing the details of any of the things in your line of vision, your mind will start to relax and you will experience an absence of separation between the perceived external objects and the perceiving or experiencing cognition. Whereas we normally think that externally perceived objects and the perceiving cognition are inherently separate, that the one is out there and the other is in here, nevertheless, when you relax your vision in this way and simply look without concepts at appearances, then in your experience at that time, there will be no distinction between the apprehended objects and the apprehending cognition. There are still appearances, you are still physically seeing things, but there is no fixated apprehending of them.

So look directly at the object, but without examining it or particularly attending to its characteristics, and don't be too outwardly focused on the object. You don't need to stare at it wide-eyed. Look at your experience of the object and simply see the insubstantiality, the emptiness of the experience.

Having directed your attention to the experience of the object of visual perception, then relax slightly, and then look again. By alternating relaxation and attention to the experience of the object, you can continually examine that experience, by looking at it directly. In the same way, you can apply this technique to the other sense consciousnesses, to the experience of sound, of smell, of taste, and of tactile sensations. When you do this, then you are looking at the nature of the experience of the object in each case, rather than at the characteristics of the objects themselves. You're looking to see if there is any substantiality whatsoever in the consciousness that is this experience of the appearance of the visual form or the sound or whatever it may be.

Among other things, you can look to see what are the differences, if any, between different consciousnesses of different objects. For example, is the consciousness that is generated when you see something yellow different from the consciousness that is generated when you see something red? Or, is the eye consciousness generated when you see a form different from the ear consciousness that is generated when you hear a sound? Of course, they are different in the coarse sense that one is an eye consciousness and the other is an ear consciousness. But is the nature of the mind or consciousness that experiences these two types of objects fundamentally different?

As you apply this technique, you are not really looking at the object. You are looking at that which experiences the object. You can also look to see where that consciousness arises. Does it come from anywhere? Does it abide anywhere? Does it go anywhere? If you come to the conclusion that it arises in such and such a way and goes somewhere else or disappears in such and such a way, that is probably conceptual. You have to look very directly. It can't be a matter of speculation or reasoning. This is very different from analyzing sense perception and thinking that this consciousness must arise from these causes and conditions and must dissolve in such and such a way. It's a matter of looking directly at the consciousness that experiences.

When you're looking at the consciousnesses that experience these external appearances, then you're experiencing the essential emptiness of that consciousness. You do this by looking at the consciousness to see if it has any substantiality. For example, if I'm taking this vase as the objective support for the technique, then what is happening is that I am generating an eye consciousness of the vase. With regard to the eye consciousness that is generated in bringing together my eyes and the vase I see: where exactly is this consciousness generated? Does this consciousness arise in the vase? Does the consciousness arise in my eyes? Does it arise somewhere in between them? If it arises in between them, does it actually fill the distance between the vase and my eyes? Or is it less substantial than this? Is it insubstantial? These are the kinds of things to be looked at.

That is working with outer or external appearances.

Working with Internal Appearances

In working with internal appearances you are working with the sensations that arise for you internally and all the things that appear to your mind— the forms and sounds and so forth—as mental perceptions, and all the other things that arise in your mind. Previously, when you looked at the mind within stillness and occurrence you were looking at what you would normally regard to be the internal or subjective aspect of mind, the mind that experiences. Here, although really there is no ultimate distinction between the internal cognition and the externally experienced object, in this technique of looking at the mind amidst appearances you would probably say you were looking at what appears to be the external, objectively appearing aspect of mind. You are looking at appearances that appear to the mind, rather than looking at the mind to which they appear. Ultimately, of course, these two are not two different things, but in our normal and confused way of perceiving them they do appear to be. Here you are concerned with forms and sounds and pleasure and pain, and so forth, all of the things that you experience. In other words, you are looking at the experienced aspect rather than the experiencing aspect. Nevertheless, if you look at these directly, in a relaxed way and without concept, then there will be no fixated apprehension of the characteristics of appearance, and in that way, while the appearances themselves will not cease, they will not be a cause of further fixation because there is no fixated apprehension of them to begin with. And as you look you discover that you can directly experience the nature of this consciousness, yet it is beyond being apprehended either as existing or as non-existing. And the recognition that this consciousness is beyond any kind of imputation of existence or non-existence is cutting through the fixation on either its solidity or its utter non-existence.

When you look at these things, again don't let this become a logical analysis of sense perception; don't try to deduce or infer how it must be. Try to experience it directly. Then, when you pursue this process of directly looking at sense experience, you will resolve that appearances are inseparable from the mind that experiences them, and that the imputed objective aspect of appearances has no existence beyond the experience itself. Therefore the nature of what we ordinarily impute to be an objective aspect of experience, as an appearance or a phenomenon separate and distinct from the subjective cognition of it, is in fact not separate from it. And the nature of the experience in which the cognition and the object are really inseparable is the unity of the appearance, or experience, and its emptiness.

When you look at the object, if it seems to you that the object is vividly out there—it's vividly or obviously out there and separate from you—then look to see, is there something that exists separate from the object that thinks the object is out there? By looking in that way, you'll find that, while the appearance of the object is unimpeded (in other words, is present and vivid), there is nothing in the experience that exists apart from that object which would let you say that the object exists apart from it. While the vividness of the experience itself is pervasive and penetrating, there's nothing other than the vividness of the experience itself. When you recognize the non-duality of mind and appearance, then you will cease to fixate on the mind that is viewing the object as having any existence separate from the object. Any fixation on that mind as being a perceiver outside or beyond the object simply vanishes.

Five Ways to Look at Mind within Appearances

In this technique, as in the previous ones, there are several subdivisions of ways that you look at the mind within appearances. The first is to examine the relationship between your mind and the objects that appear to it. Whether we are speaking of the sensations that appear in your mind or the objects that appear, supposedly, externally to the mind, in either case, you have an experiencing cognition and an experienced object. The first way of looking at the mind within appearances is to look at whether this experiencing cognition and what it experiences are the same or different. You should not let this become an exercise in logical reasoning; you are not attempting to analyze the situation and determine this through thinking about it. What you are looking at is: When you are experiencing an appearance, is that appearance truly separate from you, in other words, is it separate from the experiencing mind? How do you experience it? Do you experience the mind and what it experiences as different, or as the same? The second way of looking at the mind within appearances is related to that. If appearances are in some way separate from the mind, then how do they arise within the mind? Do they arise in the mind like a reflection arising on the surface of a mirror? Or is the mind projecting outward as an appearance? In other words, when objects appear to you—principally here externally apparent objects—is it the case that the appearances come into and enter your mind, or that the mind somehow goes out and enters into appearances, and if they're separate, what is the meeting point between the appearances and the experiencing mind? Which of these is the case? Again, this should be looked at experientially and not analytically.

Do appearances come into the mind or does mind go out to and enter into appearances are the second and third ways of looking at the mind within appearances. The fourth way, with regard to this inseparability of mind and appearance, which you may have discovered—where, although there is the appearance of a subject and an object, you may nevertheless be experiencing them as inseparable—is: Do you experience this as nonexistent objects that nevertheless appear and a nonexistent cognition that nevertheless experiences these objects? Do you experience this in that way as a unity of appearance and emptiness?

The fifth part of the technique concerns another type of experience: You observe that, while objects that appear to you do not cease to appear—even when you look at them in this way—in experiencing them without fixation you observe that, while appearing, they are nevertheless empty of true, inherent, or independent existence. When you look inward at this mind that experiences these objects, you discover that, although your mind experiences these appearances, that mind itself has no substantial existence as any "thing" or being anywhere at all. In that way, although there is the continued experience of appearances, you are without fixation on any supposed existence or reality to either the apparent objects, or the apparent subjective cognition. You experience an absence of a viewing mind and an absence of an inherently existent viewed object. Nevertheless there is the continued appearance or experience of apparent objects by the mind. In this way, it is said that appearances appear while being empty and remain empty while appearing, which is what is meant by saying that they are a unity of appearance and emptiness. This way of looking at appearances, the traditional image for this, is said to be like the way a small child will look at the images in a temple when it enters that temple. The child has no fixated apprehension of one thing or another. In this case, we're talking about a Vajrayana temple that's full of things, such as statues and images of lineage gurus and yidams, offering utensils and thangkas. If we were to enter into the temple, we would say, "Here is a statue of so and so, here is an offering bowl," and so on. But a very small child would not identify any of these things nor be able to name them. Yet, at the same time, the child would see everything perfectly clearly; they would see exactly what we see, but without superimposing a conceptual designation of things as being this or that. Similarly, in the mahamudra recognition of sense perception, there is the same pure experience. Not only is there no fixation on the object being separate from the mind or on the mind being separate from the object, but there isn't even any fixation on a substantial thinker who thinks that these two aren't separate from one another. This fifth point is to look to see whether this is how you experience it or not.

From the point of view not of meditation practice, but of reasoning, it can be determined that all the things that appear to us are of the nature of our mind, and also that the mind itself is obviously of the nature of the mind itself. Normally when we think about things we regard that which appears to us externally as composed of particles, and therefore as made up of matter, and we regard our cognition or our mind as a mere cognitive clarity or awareness and therefore as fundamentally different in nature from what we experience or what appears to us. But if we analyze carefully how we experience, we will see that what appears to us are actually fixated images created by our minds through taking many things together and designating them as units with certain designated characteristics. If you analyze the objective bases in physical reality for these designated images — and it is the designated images which we experience, not the objective bases — then you determine that the objective bases themselves, while apparently composed of particles, are actually composed of particles that when analyzed [in greater and greater detail] to the end, eventually disappear under analysis, and end up being composed of nothing. Nevertheless, appearances do appear to us. This of course is about reasoning and not about meditation; this is not an exercise for meditation.

Why then, if this is how things are, if the appearances that we experience are merely designated, fixated images based upon taking things as lump sum, why do we experience these things as externally existent and separate from ourselves? Simply, because appearances appear to our mind, we assume that they have an existence separate from our mind. Because we see something, we assert or assume that it exists. We never assert the existence of something we have to perceive. The basic argument that we always use for asserting the existence of something is that we perceive it. Nevertheless, given the way we perceive things, when we perceive things, we are really perceiving mental images, so, therefore, since there is no way to say that anything exists other than having the reason that you perceive it, and since everything you perceive is by definition, in fact, cognition perceiving its own clarity in the form of these fixated images, then as was said by Dharmakirti, "Everything you experience is really just cognitive clarity, or cognitive lucidity."

Nevertheless, many of the things that appear to us as external objects, such as rocks and mountains and trees, and so on, seem very solid, very independent, and one might ask, "How can we assert that such things are mental appearances?" For example, when you dream of rocks and mountains and trees, these things are very vivid and seem quite external to you and yet they are not external to you; they are simply mental images and mental appearances. The reason why those specific mental images arise in that specific dream is the force of habit. In the same way, the reason why a given being experiences the world in their particular way is because of their particular habit. Things are not really external to the perceiver. They are experienced as though they were external to the perceiver through the power of that perceiver's habit. In this way it is taught that appearances are mind.

Pursuing this kind of reasoning, which establishes that appearances are mind, will lead to certainty about this. If it does lead to certainty, then you can rest within this certainty in your meditation, and there will arise some experience in the meditation of the absence of inherent existence of external appearances—the unity of mind and appearances, and so on. This may arise from time to time. However, you should not be discouraged if you find that you cannot generate any resolution or certainty about the mental nature of appearances. It may be helpful to use the distinction that was proclaimed by the omniscient Longchenpa when he said, "Appearances are mind, but apparent objects are not mind." The distinction he was making was between appearances—the actual subjective experience of a thing, such as the internal mental experiences—and the external objects that generate appearance.[38] Therefore it may be helpful to limit the training of your mind within appearances to those things that are clearly subjective appearances. For example, if you use those things that clearly appear to you as mental phenomena, such as sensations, emotional states, and so on, then you can still use these for training the mind within appearances and [at the same time] you will not be troubled by the inability to resolve whether [external] appearances are mind.

Of the three techniques we've looked at — looking at the mind within stillness, within occurrence, and within appearances — the first two were somewhat easier to understand and to apply, because they were concerned with experience that we easily recognize as occurring within the mind. The problem we face with the third technique, which makes it a little more difficult, is that we have a very strong habit of considering sense perception to be an experience of something outside the mind. Nonetheless, when you perceive something, when you, for example, look directly at the consciousness that is the actual experience of seeing that form, you realize that that consciousness, while clear and vivid, is at the same time utterly insubstantial; it has no solidity, no location, nor any other kind of substantiality. You'll never find those qualities. If you can discover the same nature of mind that we looked at in the earlier techniques, the same unity of lucidity and emptiness, in the context of the experience of appearances, this will enhance your recognition of the mind.

Pointing Out Appearances

That was viewing the mind within appearances. Next is pointing out the mind within appearances, and this is a presentation of what is an authentic experience of the relationship between mind and appearances. When you are meditating and looking at the mind within appearances, then you may have the experience that, while the perceived objects and the perceiving mind do not seem in any way to disappear or cease to exist and are, in a sense, still present, when you actively look at them, you do not find anything in either that exists separate from the other. And in that way, when looking at the mind that experiences appearances, you find that there is nothing in that mind to fix upon as a truly existent subject or apprehender, yet the mind still appears to experience. And when you look at the perceived objects, while they do not disappear and while you are looking at them, they remain vivid appearances that are without anything in them anywhere that you can fix upon as existing separate from the experience of the non-duality of appearances and mind. This non-duality of appearance and mind is held to be the authentic experience or recognition of the mind within appearances.

Questions

Question: Rinpoche, earlier you seemed to say that some objects are exempt from being appearances that appear to the mind. You were talking about appearances, and then you were talking about apparent objects as not being part of that same sort of scheme. You seemed to be saying that there is something beyond mind, [apparent objects] that are not subject to the rules of karma, that would be permanent, in effect.

Thrangu Rinpoche: The statement by Longchenpa, that appearances are mind, but the objects that appear are not mind, is regarded as a concession to the difficulty of recognizing that apparent objects are mind. It is not regarded here as a definitive statement that only subjective appearances are mind and the other things are not. It is a concession to the difficulty we have with recognizing that all things are nothing other than mind. As a concession to that difficulty, and as a step to realizing that [all appearances, subjective and objective, are merely mind], you are given this distinction between subjective appearances and apparent objects. Apparent objects are things that appear to you as external to yourself, and appearances are your internal experiences of things, such as your sensations, physical and mental. The reason why this distinction is made is that when you are meditating it is easy to work with the internal appearances and to recognize their nature and to use them as a basis for the recognition of the mind. It is harder to work with external appearances. It is easy to determine the mental nature of external appearances using reasoning, but it is difficult to experience it directly in meditation. Therefore it is suggested to emphasize using the internal appearances as objects for meditation.

Question: Rinpoche, my question is very closely related to the first one, but I guess I would ask it a little bit differently. At some point you said to us that, if we came to believe that when we no longer exist or we seem to die that things do not go on, that would be a fallacy. I think that is what I understood. I guess my question is, if I understand your response to the last question, we are working toward understanding that even the things that appear external and hard and solid like rocks and trees are also the fabrication of our mind. We just use the internal things, as you said, to begin with, because it is easier for us to work with that than to actually come to experience the mental nature of external objects. We may understand intellectually, but to experience that the tree is also totally a fabrication would be difficult. First, I want to know if I understood you correctly, that indeed we are eventually going to come to the realization that everything is mind, including the things that seem most solid. And then the second part of my question is, when the world appears to continue, and I guess it does, when we die, if it does, is this again just because others have the same mental habits, or very similar mental habits to those, let's say, that I have? So they'll still see the rocks and trees when I perhaps go through the bardo and experience something totally different and perhaps come out on the other side in another realm altogether?

Rinpoche: As for your first question, yes, you understood correctly. Finally one has to resolve that even apparent objects are not other than mind. With regard to your second question, the reason why, in the experience of others, the appearances of the world do not stop when a given person passes away is that the similar experiences of others are produced by karma similar to that which produced the experiences of the person who passed away. For example, when several different people see much the same thing, they see much the same thing because they have accumulated much the same karma. However, they are each seeing it individually. Everyone's experience is individual, as similar as it may be to that of others. It is like, for example, placing a vase on a table and a hundred mirrors around it. Each of those mirrors will reflect the image of the same vase, but each is yet a distinct image of that vase.

Question: When experiencing the perception of so-called outer objects, when in that state where the perceiver and the object are one and there's no longer a sense of there being a perceiver, is there a danger there of being too open to negative influences?

Rinpoche: Generally speaking, when we have this experience as beginners of the mixing of subject and object, or the non-duality of subject and object, it occurs only in meditation, which means that you're probably sitting in a safe place. It does not occur for beginners in post-meditation, so it doesn't become a problem. Now, when we say beginners, we mean those practicing the first half of the mahamudra path, the two yogas of one-pointedness and beyond elaboration. It's only at the levels of one taste and non-meditation that this could start to occur in post-meditation. But at those levels, when this occurs, the vividness or clarity of the unimpeded appearances themselves are undiminished by the absence of a subject-object duality. And so, because the appearances are undiminished, the distinct experience of the various characteristics of the appearance is undiminished, so the person is not in any danger. The only thing that is diminished by the absence of a subject-object duality is the pain and pleasure which we normally associate with appearances

Question: Rinpoche, in our practice, we've talked about three ways of coming to understand the mind; and in our practice, is it better to pick one of those ways and work steadily on that until we make real progress, or to use all three?

Rinpoche: Well, if you can, the best way to deal with it is to begin with looking at the mind within stillness and practice that until you fully resolve the nature of the mind in that context. Then look at the mind within occurrence — again, until that's resolved — and then look at the mind within appearances, and so on.

Question. Rinpoche, if, in reality, thoughts are self-liberated as they arise, are there two types of thoughts, those that are real and unreal (in that, not recognized as self-liberated, thoughts are unreal), or do thoughts naturally arise as self-liberated and then we imprison them, or something? Because we don't seem to recognize that thoughts actually are self-liberated as they arise. In other words, is self-liberation the nature of all thoughts, or does self-liberation only occur if we recognize the nature of thoughts?

Rinpoche: Self-liberation and liberation upon arising are not characteristics of thought; they are what happens when the nature of thought is recognized. So it's not the case that you either recognize the self-liberation or don't; self-liberation is the result of recognition. Normally, thoughts are anything but self-liberated. A thought arises, and it takes us over, and that produces another thought, and so on. On the basis of these thoughts, we generate further confused projections, on the basis of which we experience pleasure and pain. Now, when the nature of a thought is recognized, what happens to that thought is very much like, as is traditionally said, what happens when a snake untangles or unties the knots it's tied itself into. The snake does it itself; no one has to come along and help the snake out. In the same way, when you look at the thought directly, for example, a thought of anger, and you see its nature, then the thought does not generate a further thought; the anger is not prolonged. As soon as the nature is seen, at that moment, the poisonous quality of the anger just disappears and dissolves; and that is self-liberation or liberation upon arising.

Question. Rinpoche, if one doesn't have a lot of time to meditate, is it possible just to do types two and three, looking at the mind in occurence and looking at the mind in appearances in post-meditation?

Rinpoche: If you can, that's fine. But the normal way this is done is that, in meditation practice, you generate an experience, on the basis especially of looking at the mind within stillness and then within occurrence. You generate an experience of the mind's nature, which you then attempt to bring into post-meditation and other types of experiences.

Question: I was wondering, do we all create the world of appearance, and maintain it through eons of mental habit?

Rinpoche: The appearances of the world and the maintenance of these appearances both come from various types of habit. There are varieties of what we call habitual patterns or habitual imprints, including the imprint of our actions and the imprint of our habituation to certain ways of experiencing, certain ways of seeing. And all of these various types of habitual patterns are imprinted on the alaya consciousness, the eighth consciousness. Having been placed there, they are subsequently projected outwards as experience, or they arise or appear as experience. Those that are stable will arise as stable or relatively unchanging appearances. Those that are unstable will change. Generally speaking, one type of karma is what are called shared appearances resulting from shared actions, which means that beings that have accumulated either an identical action or very similar actions will reap the result of experiencing the world in identical or similar ways, and will thereby be able to communicate and agree upon what they experience.

Question: Do we generate these appearances for play or for the evolution of compassion?

Rinpoche: Our projection of these appearances is entirely unintentional; we neither do it intentionally as play nor intentionally in order to develop compassion. In fact, it's beyond our control. We project out of confusion. It's like a fire that gets out of control and then just keeps on burning everything in its path. All of the things that happen in the world, such as the physical elements of fire or of water and of earth in the case of earthquakes and floods and so on, are karmic projections that happen beyond our control. We don't intend to bring them about but they result from actions. But there's no plan.

Question: How did the fire get started?

Rinpoche: Any of these appearances, even though they affect many different people, are experienced individually by each person who experiences them.

And the individual experience that you have is the result of your own previous actions. The connection between these individual experiences, the commonly shared appearance, which is nevertheless experienced individually by individual perspectives, is the result of the type of conceptuality that has been generated by all of the beings who will experience it. For example, an earthquake or hurricane that kills thousands of people is experienced in different ways by everyone involved, from the people who are killed to the people who hear about it on the radio or read about it in the newspaper. Every person's experience of it is particular to him or her and corresponds to their involvement in the actions and conceptuality that produce that particular type of appearance. In general, the violent agitation and destruction of the elements is produced by violent thoughts, such as thoughts like, "Kill 'em," "Bust 'em up," "Do 'em in." When lots of people have lots of thoughts like, "Let's get 'em," then you get earthquakes and hurricanes and other such things.

Question: So we start the "fires" with our own ignorance and confusion. Then I'm wondering, why do we go through this process? I know the goal is enlightenment in the end, but what does it matter?

Rinpoche: The reason for all of these appearances is our habit. Appearances always arise from habit that causes you to generate or project those particular appearances. It's a lot like dreaming. So, to use a dream as an example, when you start to dream, the dream begins as a thought, like one you would have in the daytime. But you're asleep, so the thought intensifies and becomes something like talk or gossip, and then the gossip intensifies or solidifies into images, and then you really think that you're seeing people, seeing places, going places, and so on. And that is how it works with conventional appearances as well. The basis on which these habits arise is the alaya consciousness, which we didn't get to yet; we just got through the first six consciousnesses, so I'll go through the seventh and eighth, how they work and how they generate appearances next.

Question: Thank you. I think I was really asking, now that I've listened to all these answers, why does a thought come out of nothingness? If there were just nothingness, why would a thought bother to even come out of it?

Rinpoche: You'll have to find out.

Question: Rinpoche, I was wondering: if one becomes proficient in the different levels of practice, or very good in, say, one, is it assured that we will be able to integrate that mindfulness into daily life? Or are there other skills that we need to be proficient at?

Rinpoche: Sometimes, and sometimes not, but you need to try. Gradually your ability to experience this recognition in post-meditation will expand or increase. In the beginning, it will just happen very occasionally that you'll be able to bring this recognition into post-meditation. Then it will start to happen some of the time. Then, if you keep on practicing, it will happen often. Then it will happen most of the time. But there will still be certain times or certain circumstances where it will be difficult. Eventually, you know, it expands, until it's all the time. And this is called, in the meditation language of Marpa the Translator, mixing. He talks about mixing a great deal, including mixing in conduct and mixing with the kleshas, which means bringing recognition into your daily life, into situations in which strong kleshas arise.

Question: Rinpoche, this question is in two parts. The first one has to do with the fourth and fifth techniques in the subdivision of techniques under this whole rubric of looking at appearances. What I want to know is, is it correct to link the experiences that one has in meditation to philosophical views found in the Madhyamaka traditions? Specifically, can you link the fourth experience of meditation up to the Autonomy (Svatantrika) Middle Way school, the rang gyur, and can you link the fifth experience, the fifth part of it, up to the Consequence (Prasangika) Middle Way school, the tal gyur, and would that be correct to do? That's the first part. The second part has to do with Rinpoche's statement that pursuing the reasoning will lead to [logical] certainty, and then resting in that one can generate some actual experience of that certainty. So does Rinpoche, in that connection, feel that it is useful and appropriate to practice analytical meditation as a way of preparing oneself for mahamudra, as in the tradition of other teachers?

Rinpoche: With regard to your first question, there is not any particular correlation between the fourth and the fifth parts of the technique with the Svatantrika and the Prasangika schools. These are really more talking about experiences that happen while doing this meditation. The certainty that would be generated through the logical analysis and analytical meditation on the view is a kind of a support for this practice — or could be — and would assist it. But it is not exactly correct to say that by resting in that certainty gained through analysis experience will arise. It is more the case that that certainty will give you the confidence to do the technique. The technique itself is strictly speaking independent of logical reasoning. The technique consists of looking directly at appearances; therefore it is not like a continuation of analytical meditation. On the other hand, it would certainly do no harm to familiarize yourself with the views of the Middle Way school, and so on, through pursuing analysis and analytical meditation, because they will help and inform the mahamudra view. Nevertheless, the mahamudra view itself is gained through direct experience and not through analytical meditation.

Question: Rinpoche, I do not really have any great knowledge or experience to ask a really good question. This experience of mahamudra, whatever it is, this sense of melting or dissolving or just being part of everything that happens to be, makes me feel quite raw and anxious and sad. I thought I was supposed to feel good and blissful, and I am wondering if the fear of the anxiety is what provides the glue that we are always trying to use to stick things together that are not really together, or make things appear solid that are not really solid?

Rinpoche: Exactly what kind of anxiety?

Same questioner: Well, if I were to jump into the lake in my normal state of mind I would feel that I was in the lake. But with practice, I begin to feel that I am just part of the lake and anxious about feeling a loss of boundary and just dissolving and just being part of the lake.

Rinpoche: I think that the solution to this anxiety is to clarify your understanding, because whether we meditate or not, the nature of things, dharmata, is unchanging. It is not the case that through meditating you are going to somehow bring about your own destruction. In fact, there is nothing to destroy, and through understanding the view in an intellectual way, you may be able to free yourself from this anxiety that is based on a fear of annihilation. The condition for this anxiety is probably too much fixation on your experience. And the remedy for that is to study a little bit more and understand more about the view in a conceptual way.

Same questioner: Could I ask about the remedy for the sadness, just the feeling that we are creating our own suffering and creating so much suffering with just fabricating, and so it just seems so endless? How could we possibly help others when some of us who have been practicing a long, long time are barely able to help ourselves? How could we be of genuine benefit? I guess my question is about bodhichitta.

Rinpoche: Sadness, per se, is good. As was said by Jetsun Milarepa, "Sadness is the infallible spur to diligence." The discomfort that you are describing seems to be produced by a kind of experience of emptiness, and it is because of the attitude you take toward the experience that it becomes uncomfortable. If you change your outlook or change your attitude a little bit about your experience, then this should shift things and you will not find the anxiety and the discomfort. Specifically, by coming to understand fully that there is nothing that is going to be destroyed by emptiness, then you will be free from fear; you will have more confidence in your practice. We all have this attitude that our mind, or whatever we may say our mind is, are really tiny solid things that we have to protect, and, having that attitude, then naturally when we start to have an experience of emptiness we are very threatened by it because we fear annihilation. But if you really look at your mind and you really understand it, you will see that there is not anything there that could die. There is not anything there that needs to be protected. Having that experience will shift things so that you will have confidence and no fear.

Question: I was hoping that Rinpoche might reflect upon the kind of experiences one might have if one took the opportunity to take the physical form of one's root guru as the object of appearance?

Rinpoche: It would be just the same. From this point of view it is just another appearance.

9 Looking at Body and Mind

So far, we have discussed looking at the mind within stillness, then looking at the mind within occurrence, and finally, looking at the mind
within appearances. Corresponding to these, we have gone through the identification, recognition, or pointing out of the mind within stillness, within
occurrence, and within appearances. It was said by Lord Gampopa, "The
mind itself is the co-emergent dharmakaya." This means that when you look
at the mind itself—as you do, for example, when looking at the mind within
stillness—and if you identify it as it is, you will see that it is empty, which
is to say that it has no substantial existence of any kind. However, the mind
is not merely empty; while being empty, it also is cognitive lucidity. Therefore the mind itself is the seed of the attainment of the dharmakaya, because
the mind in itself possesses the qualities and potential that will enable you to
remove all obscurations and to perfect all wisdoms.

In the next line of this quotation, Lord Gampopa says, "Appearances are
the light of the co-emergent dharmakaya," which is taking things in a slightly
different order from the one that we have been using in this text. Having
talked about the mind itself as the co-emergent dharmakaya, he then says that
the nature of appearances is that they are the light or radiance of that co-
emergent dharmakaya. Gampopa meant that the nature of appearances and
the nature of the mind that experiences them are neither the same nor different because the appearances are actually the display or expression of the
mind. The word "radiance" indicates the unlimited and unpredictable variety of expressions of the mind, which we know as appearances. This refers in
general to what we have been calling both external and internal appearances.
It is perhaps easier to see with regard to internal appearances, which are experiences within the mind that arise from the mind just as the rays of sunlight
arise from the sun. This means that this mind itself, which, as we have seen,
is empty and yet is cognitive lucidity, has a natural radiance or power to it as
cognitive lucidity. Before meditating, before recognizing things to be as they
are, one will have seen the radiance of this mind as solid external things that
are sources of pleasure and pain. But through practicing meditation, and

through coming to recognize things as they are, you will come to see that all of these appearances are merely the display or radiance or light of the mind which experiences them.

One of Gampopa's chief disciples, Dagpo Gomtsul, added to this quotation, saying, "Thoughts are the display or power of the co-emergent dharmakaya." This refers to the second way of viewing the mind and pointing out the mind's nature that we have been using—viewing the mind within occurrence. Thoughts are called the display or power of the co-emergent dharmakaya because they are a display in the sense that they move about; they are vivid and of varied occurrence. They appear suddenly, and they can change their intensity from being very intense to being very weak, and so forth; and they are of an unlimited variety in how they can appear. There are all manner of virtuous and unvirtuous thoughts. For as long as you have not meditated and have not understood the point of thoughts, then thoughts obscure and impede you, but once the nature of thoughts has been recognized and they have been seen to have no inherent existence, then thoughts neither obscure nor impede the process of meditation. While thoughts continue to manifest in their variety and change, nevertheless their nature is seen to be the dharmakaya, which is the nature of mind, and are therefore understood to be the display of the dharmakaya.

Within all three of these techniques of looking at the mind, the main concern is the mind itself, which normally we take to be "I," a self which we take to have substantial existence. The approach we are taking here is not particularly to attempt to refute these assertions, not to assert that the mind is not the self, or that it has no substantial existence. It is simply to look directly at the mind itself and, through seeing its nature to see directly that it is empty, that it is without a self. In that way, one determines the nature of the mind, the nature of the thoughts that arise [in or] around the mind, and the nature of the appearances that are the environment in which we find ourselves.

The Seventh and Eighth Consciousnesses

Previously, we looked at the first six consciousnesses: the eye consciousness, ear consciousness, nose consciousness, tongue consciousness, tactile consciousness, and mental consciousness. Five of these, the consciousnesses of the five gates or five senses, are obviously intimately connected with the physical body, as they rely upon particular organic supports in order to function. These experiences of seeing, hearing, smelling, tasting, and feeling are generated in dependence upon the physical body. Even the sixth consciousness, which is, in a sense, less physically oriented, is still intimately connected with the body in the way we experience it.

It is the seventh and eighth consciousnesses that we might take to be fundamentally different from the body. The seventh consciousness is called the consciousness that is mental affliction; the eighth consciousness is called the alaya consciousness. The eighth consciousness, the alaya, is called that because it is itself the ground of consciousness. It is that mere cognitive lucidity which is the fundamental level of consciousness.

Earlier, the terms "unstable consciousnesses" and "stable consciousnesses" were mentioned. Unstable means a consciousness that is generated when various causes and conditions come together and subsequently vanishes when those causes and conditions are no longer present together. The first six consciousnesses are like that. The seventh and eighth are stable, which does not mean permanent, but means they are continuous. They never stop functioning.

The eighth consciousness in particular, the alaya consciousness is subtle, not obvious; it never becomes more obvious, and it never simply disappears or ceases to function altogether. Nor is it permanent, because it is not the same consciousness that passes through time. For example, the alaya consciousness of last year, of last month, of yesterday, like the five consciousnesses or six consciousnesses that were generated at those times, has ceased to exist. Nevertheless, the habits of those consciousnesses and the habits of the actions performed at those times have been retained in the continuity of the alaya; therefore, in each moment, the alaya consciousness retains those habits. Eventually the results of these karmas, these actions and habits, arise or emerge as form, much like the way that, at night, when we're dreaming, the images and habits stored in the daytime emerge as dream images. What emerges from the alaya consciousness arises as both body and mind, the experience of a body and the experience of a mind.

The alaya consciousness retains the particular habits that are implanted through one's actions and habituation throughout time, as well as the beginningless habit of ignorance. All of these habits that are stored in the alaya consciousness re-emerge from it in the form of various appearances. That is how the eighth consciousness functions, how it projects appearances.

The seventh consciousness is called the consciousness which is mental affliction, or the afflicted consciousness; essentially, it is fixation on a self. The seventh consciousness is that faculty which fixates on the cognitive aspect of the alaya consciousness and mistakes it to be "I," or a self. On the basis of mistakenly fixating upon that awareness aspect of the alaya consciousness as a "self," it designates "others" as well. That's why it's called the consciousness which is mental affliction because this duality between self and other is the root of all mental affliction, or klesha. This is not the same as when we consciously think "I." That happens on the level of the sixth consciousness. The seventh consciousness is stable, which is to say, it is constant; it is always there. Whether you recollect yourself or not, whether you think of yourself or not, there is a fixation on this imputed self that is always there, whether you're eating, talking, in the midst of activity, no matter what you're doing; and it never stops.

The alaya consciousness arises as apprehended objects and an apprehending subject. The seventh consciousness fixates on the appearance of the apprehending subject as a self and, then, on the appearances of apprehended objects as other. In that way, through the action of these consciousnesses, the appearances of body and mind arise as distinct from one another, in the sense that the body appears as an apprehended object, while the mind appears as an apprehending subject. They're distinct in appearing that way, but they're not, in fact, different from one another, since they are merely two aspects of a single appearance that arises through the projection of the alaya consciousness. In that sense, as well, they are beyond being the same or different.

The Stages of Resting the Mind

All of these techniques I have been explaining involve looking directly at your mind and seeing its natural emptiness as well as its inherent clarity or lucidity. This is fundamentally the same, whether you are looking within stillness, within occurrence, within the experience of appearances, or at the relationship between body and mind. When you start to practice this, initially you will find only brief moments of recognition of the mind's nature. There will be a moment of recognition, then it will vanish; and then, later on, another moment of recognition will occur, then it will vanish; and so on. This is the first of what are called nine stages or, literally, nine methods of resting the mind (see following page), which here are applied to the resting of the mind in the recognition of its nature. The first stage is just called placement because there is an intermittent experience of placing the mind in recognition of itself and quite a bit of not placing the mind.

As you work with the practice, you will find that these intermittent moments of recognition start to lengthen slightly. There's still a lot of the time when you're not recognizing it, but the periods of recognition start to get longer, and this is called continual placement. It doesn't mean continual in the sense of unbroken or continuous, but simply more than before. However, you still have to relate to the problem that you can be distracted by thoughts; thoughts will arise and will take you out of the recognition and spin you off into following the thoughts. At this point, by exerting mindfulness and alertness, you need to intensify your return to recognition of the mind from the distraction. It is at this point, according to *Moonbeams of Mahamudra*, that the application of mindfulness and alertness has to be somewhat hardheaded; it has to have a quality of tough or uncompromising lucidity, so that there's enough clarity, enough crispness, or sharpness perhaps, to the mindfulness that you don't lose it when you try to return to the recognition.

Strengthening Mindfulness and Alertness

The faculties of mindfulness and alertness are explained in the following way in the Abhidharma: The consciousnesses that we have been talking about, whether you classify them as six or as all eight, make up one of the five aggregates, which is consciousness. One of the other aggregates, in addition to form, feeling, perception, and consciousness, is called formation. It consists principally of mental formations, or samskaras. There are various ways to classify these, the most common being fifty-one, but in any case they consist of various virtuous, unvirtuous, and neutral states that arise naturally within our mind. Among these are mindfulness and alertness, which means that they are faculties we already possess. We are not trying to create new faculties of mindfulness and alertness. What we are trying to do is apply these faculties in a specific way to extend our recognition of mind's nature. To do that, we need to intensify them, to make them a matter of conscious choice.

When we think about meditation, we tend to imagine that there is one mind that we place at rest and another mind that is somehow watching the mind at rest and protecting it from distraction. But in experience, it's not like that. In experience, what you actually do is relax your mind while looking; you relax your mind within the act of looking. By maintaining this quality of looking, you will know if you're distracted. The basic application of mindfulness and alertness, of looking within relaxation, is common to both shamatha and vipashyana. But here, in the specific context of vipashyana, it must be strengthened or intensified, so that you're never distracted, or at least so that you recognize when you are distracted, which is the function of alertness specifically. You will possess this alertness until you lose mindfulness. If mindfulness is lost, you will also lose alertness, and then it is no longer meditation; you're just as confused as you are when, normally, you forget what you're doing, what you were doing, and what you're going to do. At this point, therefore, it's necessary to increase mindfulness and alertness to the point where there is a sharpness and a toughness to their clarity. Because this is vipashyana practice, you are not merely resting the mind in a state without thought, you're resting the mind in recognition; and you're trying to be mindful not merely of placing the mind, but of placing the mind within recognition of its nature. Within those requirements, mindfulness and alertness at this point will help a great deal.

✕ Looking at the Body and Mind as the Same or Different

Returning to *Pointing Out the Dharmakaya*, we've been through three of the five techniques of looking: looking at the mind within stillness, within occurrence, and within appearance. Next, in the fourth technique, we look at and will identify the nature of the body and mind. This is called viewing the body and mind to see if they are the same or different. The function of this is to undermine and avert our fixation. Our strongest fixation and attachment are on our mind and on our body. And this is undermined and averted by demonstrating the emptiness of both. In order to demonstrate to ourselves that both the body and the mind lack inherent existence, we will look to see if they are the same or different. In the conventional context of confused appearances, we would normally regard them as distinct or as different because the mind is cognitive lucidity and the body is a physical substance. In that sense they seem fundamentally different. Therefore we would normally say that they are different because they have different characteristics or natures. The mind is cognition and the body is matter. However, this is a statement that is valid only in a relative context. Actually, our body as we know it is a mental experience; we experience it with our mind. And our mind is present in dependence upon our bodies. Thus the fourth technique consists of looking, within the meditative state, at the relationship between the body and the mind.

When you examine the relationship between your body and your mind, the first question to ask is, are they one thing, or are they two different things? If you assert that they're one thing, then you discover several differences or distinctions between them. First of all, the body is something that is born and is destroyed, while the mind is without birth and destruction. Your body starts out very small, gets bigger, then slowly falls apart, and finally ceases to be. Your mind does not. Your body is material, but your mind is a cognition. So from that point of view, it seems that they're not the same.

When we say that the body is matter, we mean that it is composed of particles. The body is composed of various parts (the head, the arms, and so on), and these are composed of their subparts (the various bones and flesh and so on), and if you keep on breaking it down, you find that the body is compounded of particles and is therefore matter. It is not a cognition. It is apparently a material thing. The mind, on the other hand, is not like that at all. The mind is mere cognitive lucidity. It is not made of particles, and it does not have parts, such as a head, hands, and so on. Furthermore, the body does not know, does not experience itself; it is the mind that experiences. For this reason as well, it seems that the body and mind are fundamentally different.

There are a number of other contradictions in the assertion that the body and the mind are the same. If the body and the mind were the same, then when the body dies, the mind should die, but we do not accept this to be the case. Again, if the body and the mind were the same, then when you stick a thorn into your body, a thorn should be stuck into your mind. And yet, when you stick a thorn into your body, there's no thorn entering your mind, it's just entering your body. For these reasons, too, it seems untenable to assert that the body and the mind are the same.

While it certainly isn't true that the mind and the body are the same, as has been shown, it also isn't true that they're different. Because, if the body and the mind are fundamentally different, then when a thorn is stuck into your body, which one experiences that? Is it the body that experiences it, or the mind? If the body and mind are different, it can only be one or the other; it can't be both. If it's only the body that experiences being stuck with a thorn, then sticking a thorn into a corpse should cause the corpse to have the experience, because, after all, it's a body. The only thing the corpse lacks is a mind. If we're asserting that it's only the body that experiences the pain of being stuck with a thorn, then it should affect a corpse just as much.

If, on the other hand, it's not the body but only the mind that experiences being stuck with a thorn because the mind and body are fundamentally different, then there is no connection between the mind and the body. Reasoning this way then not only sticking a thorn into your body but sticking a thorn into anything—into the earth, into rocks—should hurt just as much. If it's just your mind, if it has nothing to do with your body, then there's no reason why this particular body should have any particular effect on your mind that other things don't have. And yet, that's not how it is. There is a big difference between having a thorn stuck in your body and having a thorn stuck in the ground. So we can't say that the body and the mind are different, either. You can't say that the body and mind are the same, and you can't say that they are different.

Look carefully at this in meditation. The presentation we've just gone through, which is a logical analysis, is a little different from what you do when you're actually meditating. When you're meditating, look directly at the experience of your body and of your mind. Look at the way you experience your body, from the tips of the hair on your head down to the very tips of your toes, carefully looking directly at your physical experience, because you want to see what exactly is this relationship between mind and body. Mind and body seem to be somehow present, but do the body and mind actually depend upon each other, or are they fundamentally different? Reason would indicate that they're fundamentally different, and yet, when we look at our actual experience, it seems as though one cannot exist without the other. The body depends upon the mind to be experienced; the mind depends upon the body to have experience. Looking at this relationship, or dependence, is another way of coming to see the mind's nature.

So, when we look with reasoning at the relationship between the body and the mind, it seems obvious that they are different, and it does not require a great deal of argument to assert their difference. However, when we look at the relationship between body and mind from the standpoint of meditation experience, there is something to be looked at here, because we come to a different conclusion.

Also, if you look at your body, you define your body as that which is your body from the head all the way down to your toes. Now, where is your mind apart from that? Is your mind something you can point to outside the body; that is separate from the body? When you look you find that there is no mind that can be separated from the body to be pointed to. Therefore, from that point of view, you would tend to say that your mind is no different from your body, that your mind is a characteristic or quality of the body.

Also, if you look for a body that is outside of or separate from your mind, you do not seem to be able to find that either, because your identification with your body is based on the notion that this is my body, which is a notion found in your mind. Your experience of body is based on the appearance of your body to your mind. Therefore from that point of view, you would also have to say, not only is there no mind outside your body, there is no body outside of or separate from your mind.

Your body merely appears to your mind, and you also have no mind that is outside of or separate from or other than your body. There is no body outside of your mind, and yet your mind has no true or inherent existence. Therefore, your body, which must merely be a characteristic or something appearing to the mind, must have that same nature and lack inherent existence. When you experience this in meditation, it does not mean that your body disappears, but your fixation on it as solid and as a source of suffering disappears. In the practice you rest evenly in the confidence that the body is merely an appearance to your mind. This will then generate less attachment, and there will be less of a sense of solidity and of independent existence to the body, even though it will not cease to appear to you. That is how to view whether the body and mind are the same or different. Corresponding to this is the introduction to or pointing out of whether the body and mind are the same or different.

Pointing Out the Body and Mind as the Same or Different

Through looking at this again and again, you come to the conclusion that the body and the mind are neither the same nor different. They both appear, and yet in their appearance they lack true existence, because the appearance of the one depends upon the appearance of the other. In that way, while they are vivid appearances, they are vivid appearances without any inherent existence as what they appear to be. They are the unity of lucidity and emptiness, like for example, the reflection of the moon in a body of water. If you ask, "Is there a reflection of the moon in the body of water," you would have to say yes, because you see it. But if you were asked, is there actually a moon in the body of water, you would have to say no.

What is the use of experiencing this? The use is that we normally have tremendous fixation and craving for the support of our bodies, which makes us constantly threatened by what will happen to the body. We are threatened by experiences of heat and cold, hunger, thirst, and so on, and the fact that these experiences are threatening to us comes about because of our fixation on the body. We think that the body is a solid and existent thing that is somehow possessed by or hosts our mind. But if you recognize the nature of your body to be the unity of appearance and emptiness or lucidity and emptiness, then even though you will still physically feel hunger, thirst, heat, and cold, you will not be afflicted by them. They will be vivid appearances that are perceived as empty and that do not therefore bring suffering.

In the beginning, one cannot look directly at great physical sufferings such as intense sickness and not be affected by them. But one can, in the beginning, work with less intense sensations and gradually progress to the point where any physical experience can be seen through, which makes these instructions for viewing the oneness or distinctness of body and mind very useful.

That is viewing the unity or distinctness of body and mind and pointing out the unity or distinctness of body and mind. This has to be actually practiced for it to lead to its result. However, the result will be that you will be able to experience what would otherwise be intense physical suffering without its posing a problem for you, and you will also not be overpowered by physical pleasure. These will not lead to kleshas, such as arrogance, jealousy, and so on.

Questions

Question: Rinpoche, in my meditations, there seems to be some part of the mind that I call will or intention, and I'm wondering where that aspect of mind fits into what we've been talking about.

Thrangu Rinpoche: Will, or intention, is one of the fifty-one mental formations, or samskaras. Within the fifty-one, there are many subgroups. For example, the first five are called the five that are present in any cognitive situation, which are five things that have to be present for any kind of cognition. It's not one of those. It's in the next list, which is the five that serve to ascertain an object. The first of these is intention. Then there is what's called interest, then recollection (which is the same word that we often translate as mindfulness), then absorption (which is the word samadhi, but here it does not denote a profound meditative state, but a simple state of intentional cognition), and finally, prajna or knowledge, which again here doesn't denote anything profound but something that has to be present in any intentional action. So the first of the five aspects of an intentional cognitive state is obviously intention.

Question: Rinpoche, I wasn't able to distinguish clearly between what you said about mindfulness and alertness.

Rinpoche: Mindfulness is the faculty of not forgetting what to do and what not to do. That is how it's usually defined. So it means simply recollecting what you are trying to do. If we apply the term to meditation, then, in general, it's something like, "I want to bring my mind to rest; I don't want to be distracted." Usually mindfulness entails something you want to do and something you want to avoid, so you're remembering. Literally it's the same word as memory or recollection in Tibetan,

Question: It is?

Rinpoche: Yes. It is. "I remember I want my mind to rest; I don't want to be distracted." In the specific context of vipashyana, it's, "I want to recognize, and I don't want to space out." Now, in general, this is not a very stable thing. We recollect what we're trying to do one moment, and then the next moment we've flown off somewhere and we've lost it. So the application of mindfulness, the intentional application of it, is attempting to prolong the recollection or memory of what you're doing and what you're trying to do.

If you have this faculty, and to the degree to which you have this faculty of mindfulness or recollection, to that degree will you possess the second faculty of alertness, which is the awareness that knows what is occurring. It comes along with mindfulness. Alertness recognizes whether, for example, your mind is at rest or not, whether you are recognizing or not. When you are without mindfulness, you will not have any alertness. Normally, when we're not mindful, then thoughts arise and we have no recollection; there's no imposition of an intention of being aware of them, which is the recollection aspect. As a result, there is no awareness, which is the alertness aspect. Mindfulness is recollecting what you are doing, and alertness is being aware of what is occurring.

Question: Can I just take it one step further: What is meant by the term "resting in recognition?"

Rinpoche: The object that is recognized when you look at your mind is the insubstantiality of that mind (which is also, of course, what is looking). While it is an utter insubstantiality, an absence of any kind of substantial existence whatsoever; it is not a nothingness. It is an insubstantial, cognitive lucidity. This recognized object can be perceived in different ways. When you recognize the insubstantiality and you experience that insubstantiality, that's called the experience of emptiness; and when you recognize the cognitive lucidity and you experience that cognitive lucidity, that's called the experience of lucidity. But you can't really have one experience without the other. You might think you could, but in fact you can't and you aren't. This is because they are not two separate things. There is only one thing that is recognized. And in fact that which recognizes it is itself, which brings us to the question: What recognizes it? It is your own individual, self-aware awareness, recognizing itself.

Question: And that is without concept?

Rinpoche: Yes, it's without concept; it's a direct experience, and a conceptual understanding of it really has nothing to do with, and does not particularly help, that experience.

Question: I'm going to stop now, but you're talking about memory, without any concept now?

Rinpoche: Yes. I don't usually say memory, I say mindfulness because in this case, the mindfulness, or recollection, is the faculty of not wavering from the recognition. It's not a concept; it's simply the fact of not wavering.

Question. Rinpoche, when we're in the waking state, we can recall our dreams, but when we're dreaming, we normally can't recall our waking state, and therefore can't practice in a dream. And I was wondering, is there any way of extending the practice of mahamudra into the dream state, to make use of that opportunity?

Rinpoche: Yes, the dream practice within the Six Dharmas [of Naropa] is exactly that; it's a way of using dream to enhance and apply your mahamudra practice or experience.

It's a distinct training. The first thing is that there has to be stable, lucid dreaming, which means knowing that you're dreaming when you're dreaming. This is called lucid dreaming, and it has to be stabilized. Then, when you can get that stabilized, within lucid dreaming, you have to be able to recognize the emptiness within dreams. Once you're able to do that, you have to be able to rest in that throughout the dream. And it's a little tricky because, as you said yourself, you're pretty much out of it when you're dreaming. You're more out of it when you're dreaming than you are now, and we have enough trouble recognizing when we're awake.

Question: Rinpoche, I'd like to just clarify something about the practice you've been talking about. It seems that in this working with the mahamudra, initially we work with these questions that you've presented earlier as a way of clarifying or understanding our experience, and then beyond that, we continue to rest in that understanding that we've developed: non-cognitive, non-conceptual understanding Is that correct?

Rinpoche: Yes. First of all, you have to have a recognition of the nature of your mind, and as you said, the various questions and the various techniques or ways of looking, are designed to give you just that. There is also the tradition of pointing out the nature of mind, in which there's some sort of vigorous manner of causing the students to recognize it on the spot without their going through this kind of gradual investigation. This is very impressive, and often people have an experience of recognition, but soon thereafter it vanishes. The superiority of the gradual approach is that, while less dramatic initially, when you develop on your own a recognition through experience and through hard work, then you don't lose it, you know; it's because you developed it, and you get to work with it. Initially, the recognition starts to occur and is not that stable, then it's stabilized, then you gradually develop confidence in the recognition, and on the basis of confidence, you learn, through practice, through time and effort, how to rest in it. It's a gradual process, as you indicated.

Question: Rinpoche, I wasn't clear if the practice that you mentioned or described earlier deals with the seventh consciousness, or does it stay in the sixth; and then at some point, if this doesn't go into the seventh, do we actually, in mahamudra practice, address the seventh consciousness?

Rinpoche: Well, there is a connection between this technique and the seventh and eighth consciousnesses in that the object of investigation, that which is being looked at here, is projections on the part of the eighth and seventh consciousnesses. When you're looking at the relationship between body and mind, the body is projected by the eighth consciousness, and the body and mind are fundamentally fixated on as different or the same by the seventh consciousness. Nevertheless, as before, it is the sixth consciousness that performs the meditation.

10 Looking at the Stillness and Occurrence of Mind

Looking at Stillness and Occurrence as the Same or Different

W E HAVE GONE THROUGH four techniques, or ways of viewing the mind. Now we're concerned with the fifth of the five ways of viewing the mind and the corresponding fifth of the five ways of pointing out the mind's nature. Previously we saw that the first way of viewing the mind was viewing the mind within stillness, and the second was viewing the mind within occurrence. Here we look at both of them, and this way of viewing the mind is viewing the mind to see if stillness and occurrence are the same or different, or, as we also say, looking at the difference between stillness and occurrence. This is very much like the fourth technique, in which we viewed the mind to see if body and mind were the same or different. Here you are concerned with the mind, and in particular with the two states of mind, stillness and occurrence. When we think about this, and also about how things appear in general, we would say that stillness and occurrence are different, because they are distinct states of mind. When your mind is in a state of occurrence, thoughts are present and your mind is not at rest and not in a state of stillness. From that point of view it would seem obvious that these two are different. However, when you look directly at the essence of these two states of mind, then you discover that the nature of the mind within stillness and the nature of the mind within occurrence are the same. Therefore, from the point of view of how they appear, these two states could be said to be different, and from the point of view of how they really are, these two states could be said to be the same.

The first instruction in this technique is to look at the nature of your mind when it is at rest in a state of vivid lucidity and emptiness. The relationship between the mind's lucidity and its emptiness is similar to the relationship between the display of appearances and the emptiness of appearances. As has been said by many teachers with regard to appearances, and the same holds true with regard to the mind, "While something is appearing, at that same time it is empty; and at the same time it is empty, yet it appears." The relationship between the emptiness of an appearance and the appearance of that emptiness is so intimate, in fact, that we have to say it is the emptiness itself that is appearing and the appearance itself that is the emptiness. This is called the inseparability of emptiness and appearance.

The situation with your mind is the same, except that it is much easier to see directly. The lucidity of your mind is itself the emptiness of your mind; they cannot be separated. In the fifth technique, the instruction is to simply look at that lucidity-emptiness when the mind is at rest. The first part of this technique is essentially the same as the first technique, looking at the mind within stillness. The way you look at the mind should have two qualities. One is *singyewa*, which means a crispness in its clarity, and the other one is *yetewa*, which means a vivid intensity to the clarity. When you look when the mind is at rest, look in those ways.

The second part of the technique is to allow a thought to arise and then look at the nature of the experience of that thought, or, in other words, to look at the mind within occurrence. This is exactly the same process as the second technique of looking at the mind within occurrence. The difference is that here we are combining the first two techniques. As we already discussed with regard to the second technique, when a thought arises and the nature of the thought is not recognized, then one thought will lead to another, creating a continuing movement of thoughts. (What we're talking about are fully manifest thoughts, what are called the coarse thoughts, the thoughts that occupy your mind to the point where you can be aware of them). But when you look directly at the thought and apply the technique, then it is self-liberated; it dissolves.

In the fifth technique, what you're trying to do is alternate looking at the mind within stillness and looking at the mind within occurrence, so that you can see, within direct experience, whether stillness and occurrence are the same or different. By this we mean, is the mind of stillness the same as or different from the mind of occurrence? Just thinking about it, one would tend to say, they must be different; one is stillness, the other is occurrence, which seems clear. But we don't want to think about it, we want to try to experience it, to see directly whether they are the same or different.

It makes sense to say that they cannot be the same, because after all, stillness is stillness and occurrence is occurrence; they are distinct from one another. So we can't say they are identical. If we then take them to be different, we have to very precisely discover, in direct experience, what the difference is between them. When you look to see if they are different in nature, you are looking to see if their characteristics are different, what characteristics the one possesses that the other does not. Do they have any coarse characteristics that would make them different? For example, are they different colors? Is stillness one color and occurrence another color? Is stillness one shape and occurrence another shape? Or, if you feel that they don't have those kinds of substantial characteristics, are they of different natures? Are the experience of stillness and the experience of occurrence, when you look directly at them, truly distinct from one another, are they truly different? That is the basic technique or general consideration, and then specifically with regard to how they might seem to you, there are nine questions that you can ask of your experience [of stillness and occurrence] to see what these two states are really like in order to more closely ascertain the identity or difference between them.

Nine Questions

When you look to see if stillness and occurrence are different in nature, the first question is: Are they simultaneously present, yet separate, like two strings or pieces of thread put side by side? In other words, equally present and equal in degree of reality, or equal in how fundamental they are to the mind, but nevertheless separate, is that how they are? That is the first one.

The second question asks: Is the difference between them more like the relationship between the earth and a chariot? If they are distinct and separate, do they have a relationship? Do they have a relationship of supporting and supported? Is the mind of stillness like the earth, on which the mind of occurrence comes and goes like a chariot? Is stillness the environment in which occurrence occurs? For example, like the earth and the trees that grow on it. Is that what their relationship is?

The third question is: Is their difference one of alternation? If you find that they do not seem to be simultaneously present, but distinct, like two separate pieces of thread or rope, and they do not seem to be in the relationship of environment and that which is supported by that environment, then is the relationship between stillness and occurrence like two pieces of rope that are braided to form a braided rope—so that they alternate, so that when there is stillness there is not occurrence, and when there is occurrence there is no stillness? Is that how they are.

Those three questions are ways of looking at the possibility that stillness and occurrence are fundamentally different in nature. The next set of questions is concerned with the possibility that they might be fundamentally the same in nature. Again if, through looking at the mind, you come to the conclusion that they are the same, then you have to question what this sameness or oneness of stillness and occurrence means and consists of. How could they be the same? After all, occurrence is lots of activity going on in your mind, giving rise to one thought or many thoughts; while stillness is when the mind is at rest, completely settled down. How can you say those two are the same thing? If they are one, the same thing, then what do you mean by this? Do you mean one turns into the other in the sense of a piece of iron that can be changed into gold and then be changed back into iron? Is it some sort of transformation in place, is that what their oneness is? The image used here, of iron being turned into gold, refers to the story about Arya Nagarjuna, who had a lot of wealth at his disposal, for building temples and providing the sustenance for large numbers of ordained monks. If you ask where all that wealth came from, it came from his alchemical ability to turn iron into gold. Is that what happens here? Does stillness somehow get transformed or transmuted into occurrence, or vice versa? Is that what you mean by their sameness? That is the fourth question.

Or the fifth, is it the oneness of two distinct things that have been mixed to form a mixture, like mixing milk and water, where they start out different, then you pour one into the other, and they become the same? Are stillness and occurrence initially different, but then somehow they're mixed together and become identical? These questions are to be applied based on what you experience using the basic technique. If you think that stillness and occurrence are different, then you use the first three questions, and if you think that they're the same, then you question that with the next three questions.

The sixth question is concerned with experiencing a difference: Is it the case that stillness and occurrence are not mixed like water and milk, but are distinct in their characteristics, like water and waves that rise on the surface of that body of water and therefore appear in alternation, so that when there is stillness there is no occurrence and when there is occurrence there is no stillness, but that nevertheless their nature is the same stuff? Is it the case that the nature of stillness is the unity of cognitive lucidity and emptiness and that the nature of occurrence is that same unity, and that yet nevertheless they appear in alternation? That is the sixth question.

At this point, we've had six questions. The first three were concerned with regarding stillness and occurrence as fundamentally different. Then we had two questions about experiencing them as the same. Finally, the sixth question was, do you experience them as like water and waves, being of the same nature but distinct in mode or appearance?

The next three questions, the final three of this section, which sort of go together, are as follows.

If you find that the answer to the sixth question is yes, and that the nature of both stillness and occurrence is lucidity-emptiness, what exactly does this mean? You examine this further. The seventh question is: If you think that the nature of both stillness and occurrence is lucidity-emptiness, then do thoughts become this lucidity-emptiness when they are recognized? When the nature of a thought is seen, does that nature become this lucidity-emptiness? Allow a thought to arise, then get rid of it. Does the thought only become lucidity-emptiness when you get rid of it?

Or the eighth question is: When a thought just vanishes, without your doing anything to it; does it become lucidity-emptiness whether it is recognized or not, but only after it vanishes? In other words, it wasn't lucidity-emptiness before and does it only become lucidity-emptiness when it vanishes? Does the thought vanish into this state of lucidity-emptiness?

Or number nine is: Is the nature of a thought lucidity-emptiness from the moment of its inception, irrespective of its being recognized or not, or having vanished or not; is that just its basic nature?

Which of those three do you experience, if you say that both stillness and occurrence are lucidity-emptiness?

With regard to their actual nature, what you will discover when you look at stillness and occurrence in general and in these nine ways is that stillness and occurrence are distinct experiences, but nevertheless their nature is the same. Their manner of appearance, the kundzop, or relative truth, of stillness and occurrence, is that they are different. Stillness is stillness, and occurrence is occurrence. And yet, their nature, what is called in the jargon of dharma, the dondam, or absolute truth, is that they are the same.

The nature of occurrence is lucidity-emptiness; occurrence, the thoughts that move through your mind, are not things that in any way exist apart from mind and that therefore have a nature other than that lucidity-emptiness which is the mind's nature. Stillness, as well, is simply another expression of the same nature of the mind, so therefore the nature of stillness, as well, is lucidity-emptiness. Their appearances are distinct and as experiences, they occur in alternation. You can recognize a state of stillness as distinct from a state of occurrence, a state of occurrence as distinct from a state of stillness, but when you perceive the nature of either one of these, you are seeing the same thing.

While the appearances or manifestations of stillness and occurrence are distinct as experiences, they are equally lucidity-emptiness in their essential nature. For example, when you look directly at the experience of stillness, or the mind at rest, you can't find something that's resting, or its quality of resting, or what it's resting in. When the mind is at rest there is nothing that exists that is at rest and there is no place in which the mind is at rest. Nevertheless, while it is insubstantial and without inherent existence in that way, the cognitive clarity of the mind is undiminished by the mind's being at rest. Therefore, when the mind is at rest, the nature of that mind is a cognitive clarity that is empty, so it is called lucidity-emptiness. And when you look directly at an occurrence of mind, a thought, you can't find any substantiality to it anywhere. When there is the occurrence of thought within the mind, then the thoughts themselves have no inherent existence. The thoughts do not come from anywhere that truly exists, and they do not remain or disappear anywhere that truly exists. While these thoughts have an appearance of occurrence or movement, they are nevertheless simply the display of that same naked cognitive clarity which is undiminished when the mind is at rest. Therefore, these thoughts that are utterly insubstantial or without inherent existence are in themselves, in their nature, that cognitive clarity and are therefore a cognitive clarity that is empty, so they too are lucidity-emptiness. With regard to the nature of thoughts being lucidity-emptiness, it is not the case that thoughts upon their arising are solid and truly existent and only become lucidity-emptiness when they are recognized, or through some effort of meditation. Nor is it the case that thoughts only become lucidity-emptiness when they subside or when they disappear. From the moment of their inception, from the moment of their arising, all thoughts are of this nature of lucidity-emptiness. As is said in the liturgy for meditation on Guru Dorje Trolo called *Zangpupma*, "See all thoughts as the wind moving through space." Of course we can detect the movement of the wind through space, but it has no solidity and it has no beginning and end. In the same way, thoughts do not come from anywhere; they are not present anywhere; they do not go anywhere and they have, themselves, no substantial entity or no substantial existence. Therefore thoughts, like the mind at rest, or thoughts, like the mind in occurrence, are naked lucidity-emptiness. If you practice this meditation, then you will definitely come to this experience and recognition.

How to Practice

There are two ways to use the nine questions. One is to think about them and determine, through reasoning, that this is how things must be; the other way is to use them as techniques for gaining actual meditation experience. You must not confuse these two processes. Developing an understanding through thinking about the questions is entirely different from generating direct experience of what these questions are trying to provoke. It is of no use in generating actual experience, and may, in fact, prevent it. You must go through the process; whether or not you understand these things intellectually, you must go through the questioning to gain direct experience.

Those are the five ways of looking at your mind that are presented in the text. You can think of them as five ways of looking or five views, since we're using view here to mean looking directly. The key to all of them is to look openly and without preconception, without deciding what you're going to find when you look. Don't be clever. Don't try to strategize, by thinking, "Well, I need to see this, so maybe I can try to make it happen." Don't tilt —this is taking a bit of a liberty in translation, but it captures the meaning —as when you play pinball, and you try to cheat by tilting. Don't tilt. This means, don't think, "I need to see it; I've got to experience emptiness. What I'm experiencing is not what I want, so I've got to get rid of it and experience something else." You have to have a completely open mind about what things mean. You may have an image of emptiness, or a conceptual approximation of lucidity, but don't inflict these ideas on your experience.

If you can diligently cultivate these ways of looking directly at mind and look openly at your own experience, you can stick to them without trying to talk yourself into some sort of profound realization and without being attached to your intellectual understanding of the experience, then you will see your mind's nature.

Four Recognitions

Following this section in the text there are four additional introductions. The first of these is the pointing out that appearances are mind, and this is connected to some extent with the previous practice, the third practice, which involves determining the sameness or difference of appearances and mind. Through doing that practice, in the beginning, you will come to a resolution that the internal appearances, mental experiences, are nothing other than mind, and eventually you will come to the recognition that even external appearances are nothing other than mind. In any case, the recognition that no appearance whatsoever exists beyond the mind is the identification of appearances as mind.

Having recognized that all that appears is the display of the mind, then it is necessary to recognize the nature of that mind. In order to do this you use the first two techniques: looking at the mind within stillness and looking at the mind within occurrence. Through looking at the mind in these two situations, you discover that the mind has no origin, has no location, and has no destination. You experience states of stillness and occurrence, but nothing in these states has any origin, location, or destination, and you discover that there is nothing that is still in stillness and nothing that is moving in the state of occurrence. This recognition that these states which are distinct —or lucid or vivid in their appearances—are nevertheless utterly empty is the second recognition, the recognition that mind is emptiness.

Having recognized that appearances are mind and that mind is emptiness, does this recognition that mind is emptiness mean that mind ceases? Upon this recognition does mind cease to exist, like a candle being snuffed out? Of course it does not. Because while mind is emptiness, the display of this emptiness that is mind's nature is unceasing and unlimited in its variety. The emptiness that is the nature of mind is not an absolute nothingness, not a dead, blank, static emptiness. It is an emptiness that is at the same time an unimpeded or unceasing and unlimited display of cognitive lucidity. In short, the emptiness of mind itself is at the same time its capacity to arise in experience, its capacity to exhibit its display. So the third recognition is the recognition that emptiness is spontaneous presence. Now here in the texts this is referred to as the recognition that the gleam or light or display of that emptiness that is the mind's nature is of an unceasing and unlimited variety, of which the nature is great bliss, or mahasukha. The reason why this statement is made is that through recognizing that appearances are mind and that mind is emptiness, you become free from fixation upon the reality of substantial things and upon the fixation upon the identification of the imputed self with some part of these substantial things. As long as you have this fixation on substantial reality and a fixation on a self, of course you suffer, because these fixations are the cause of suffering. So in the absence of these fixations, when in contrast to those fixations you experience the display of emptiness as it is, as a spontaneous presence that is not substantial entities and is not a self, then rather than this causing suffering, this produces great bliss. Therefore this is the third recognition, the recognition of emptiness as spontaneous presence.

The recognition of emptiness as spontaneous presence is very important, because normally when we think of emptiness, or even use the word emptiness, we have an idea of nothingness, of nothing whatsoever. Of course our meditation on emptiness is by no means a meditation on nothingness, a meditation on nothing whatsoever. If we attempted to cultivate this state of nothingness, that would be the cultivation of a nihilistic view. Mind of course is empty, but the emptiness of mind is a capacity for display, a capacity for an infinite variety of unlimited and unceasing display. Therefore this emptiness of mind is spontaneous presence; it is not an incapacity for display. Therefore, because this emptiness is a capacity for spontaneously present display, then, when this is fully revealed, upon obtaining awakening, you do not become an idiot; you become infinitely wise. A Buddha is not an idiot, a Buddha sees all things exactly as they are, and is fully capable of engaging in unlimited activity for the benefit of beings. The reason why a Buddha has these qualities is that emptiness is spontaneous presence. However, you might wonder: If emptiness is spontaneous presence, in other words, if the display of emptiness is unceasing even after it has been recognized, does that mean that that display will continue to manifest as kleshas and suffering as it does now in the unrecognized state? The answer is no, because when the nature of this display is recognized to be as it is, to be the spontaneous present display of emptiness, then that display is self-liberated, which means that when thoughts arise and their nature is recognized, then simultaneously with their arising they are already freed, they are already liberated, they bring no fixation. Therefore the <u>fourth introduction</u> is pointing out spontaneous presence to be self-liberation. Self-liberation here is like the fact that a snake no matter how many knots it ties itself into can untie the knots by itself. Someone does not have to come along and help the snake out. The snake can uncoil itself, can untie itself. In the same way, when the nature of thoughts and so forth is recognized, then the thoughts arise already liberated. They do not bring up further fixation.

Although the nature of the mind never changes, because we have habits that have accrued over a period of time without beginning, our experience of meditation will fluctuate. Sometimes, even though we do not have realization, it will seem that we have realization. Sometimes, even though things are going well, the meditation will seem to be terrible and pointless. Also, it is common to generate a great deal of hope and anxiety about the progress of meditation. We tend to hope that our meditation will go well and that we will have good and profound experience, and we tend to fear that it will go poorly or badly. Hope and fear are irrelevant in the practice of meditation because in this practice of meditation you are not attempting to create anything new. You are merely trying to observe, just as it is, what is already there, so you need not have any anxiety with regard to what you experience while making that observation. You simply just look and rest in seeing whatever you see, and you do not have to hope to see one or the other.

Questions

Question: Can I also use the techniques during visualization?

Thrangu Rinpoche: Yes, you can; you can actually have a good experience of the mind at rest and the mind in movement during visualization. Also you can use the clarity, which is promoted by the visualization, to see the nature of the mind that is generating that clarity. So visualization can be used to enhance this practice.

Question: Rinpoche, with respect to the experience of kleshas in meditation, Western students are generally given at least three kinds of techniques. One is the labelling technique that goes with shamatha, one is the taking and sending that comes with tonglen and relative bodhichitta practice, and one is this kind of vipashyana mahamudra approach. I wonder if Rinpoche would say something about how to co-ordinate these various approaches to encountering kleshas in one's meditation, and also in one's post-meditation.

Rinpoche: Labelling and tonglen and the mahamudra approach to recognition of mind's nature need to be applied not so much depending upon what level you're at, but simply apply what works in a specific situation. To some extent, it depends upon the actual strength or intensity of the klesha that has arisen. You may be able to use the mahamudra approach with a certain level of intensity, but you may be swept away by something that passes a certain ceiling of intensity. There is a specific technique that's recommended for extremely strong kleshas which is called, literally, distancing. It begins with what you would call labelling, which is the recognition of the klesha arising as opposed to the recognition of the nature. Then you "disown" the klesha by reminding yourself of how much trouble it's going to cause you and how you don't want that. The reason this distancing is so important is that a lot of the power of kleshas comes from the fact that they seduce you into thinking that you need them. When anger arises, what maintains the anger is the sense, "I need this anger, this anger is right, it's appropriate, it's necessary." If you can shake off that belief that the anger is appropriate and necessary, which is called distancing, then you are not afflicted by it. It's the same with other kleshas, for example, attachment. When you feel attached to something, a lot of the attachment consists of feeling you should be attached, that you want to be attached. distancing cuts through that.

However, the basis for any way of relating to the kleshas is some kind of recognition, and ideally, if you can, you'll want to use the mahamudra approach of looking directly at the nature of the klesha, recognizing its nature. If you can't do that in a specific situation, then you should apply one of the other two approaches, in this case, distancing which is coordinated with labelling. Of course, there's also the approach of taking and sending, or tonglen, which is called transforming the klesha into wishing others well

Question: Rinpoche, I'm trying to establish the importance of view. When we are practicing and using the techniques, asking the nine questions that you just talked about, how important is the view in the context of conduct, in the context of aspiration and application? Is it essential to cultivate the four immeasurable virtues or the six paramitas or other aspects of the bodhisattva way of conduct, before one can actually realize the mind's nature?

Rinpoche: It is not necessarily true that one must cultivate the four immeasurables or practice the six perfections (paramita) before cultivating the recognition of mind's nature. However, at the same time, we need a pure motivation for any aspect of our practice, and the pure motivation depends upon some degree of cultivation of the four immeasurables. But it's uncertain whether you need to have perfected this before there can be any recognition. It could precede recognition, or they could be cultivated simultaneously. With regard to the six perfections, these are principally the aspect of accumulating merit, and merit is a necessary condition for practice and realization and to enhance your experience in realization. But again, one can't say with certainty that the practice of these has to precede the generation of a recognition; it has to be part of the process.

Question: Rinpoche, it's difficult not to have thoughts when I'm investigating the nature of my mind. They come up so quickly. I have two questions. One is, if a thought arises, how do you get rid of it? And number two is, how do I deal with one particular thought that arises quickly and has to do with the very quick assumption that it's like water and waves. I have years and years of belief in this. It seems almost hopeless.

Rinpoche: In any case, no matter what the thought is, don't try to get rid of it, just look right into its nature. In other words, look directly at it, at the thought, rather than the content of the thought. This is the second technique, looking at occurrence. If you look directly at it, then you will be able, through direct experience, to transcend this concept you have about water and waves. Because the analogy is limited, you know. In a sense, thoughts are like waves on the surface of a body of water, but unlike waves, they don't have a substance, they don't have a specific origin or source, and you'll see that. You'll experience that directly, at which point the thought or concept or belief about them will become irrelevant.

Question: Rinpoche, although with the realization of mahamudra as it has been described, one achieves a direct experience or discovers or recognize this nature of the inseparability of bliss-emptiness, yet at the same time one may have a direct experience of suffering and also may be following the path of compassion, which would make one sensitive to the suffering of others, and in fact, one's whole life could be dedicated to helping others and recognizing their suffering. What I would ask for is a way of understanding how the recognition of the immeasurable suffering of sentient beings is related to the recognition of bliss-emptiness.

Rinpoche: Usually we regard compassion as a state of misery, because you see the sufferings of others and you cannot do anything about it, and that makes you miserable. But the compassion that arises through the recognition or realization of mahamudra is not a state of misery; it is actually a state of great bliss. As is said in the *Aspiration Prayer of Mahamudra,* "At the moment of kindness, emptiness arises nakedly." The compassion that arises out of mahamudra ensues upon the recognition of emptiness, but at the very moment at which compassion arises, there is also further experience of emptiness itself. In particular, because of the realization from which this compassion ensues you see exactly how beings could, can, and will be liberated. You see exactly how you could help beings and exactly how beings can come to the same realization. Therefore it is not a compassion of hopelessness; it is a compassion of great optimism. While from one point of view we would consider compassion a type of sadness or characterized by sadness, in the case of the compassion of mahamudra, because of the tremendous confidence that your realization gives you, confidence not only in your own realization, but in the possibility of realization on the part of all beings, then compassion is also regarded as bliss.

Same questioner: Thank you. Could I ask just one further question to clarify it? Why, at the recognition of bliss-emptiness mahamudra realization, would compassion at that moment arise? What is the logic or progression there?

Rinpoche: As was said by the Third Gyalwa Karmapa in his mahamudra aspiration, "The nature of beings is always Buddha," which means that when you recognize the nature of things, which includes the nature of beings, you recognize that there is no intrinsic need for beings to suffer. Therefore you see that the nature of your realization and the nature of the suffering of beings is the same, but because beings do not have that realization, they are in [a seemingly] endless experience of samsara. When you realize the nature of all things, you also realize at the same time that all beings could have that realization too but do not, and that knowledge automatically produces tremendous compassion. Again, it is not an impotent compassion, because you also recognize how to help beings, or lead beings to that realization.

For example, if you consider individuals like Naropa, Marpa, and Milarepa, who realized mahamudra, and compare their mind and our mind, it is not the case that their mind is inherently superior. It is not the case that there is some reason why they are inherently or intrinsically capable of realizing what they realize and why we beings are intrinsically incapable of it. That is not the case at all. The nature of their mind and the nature of our mind is exactly the same. The only difference is that they realized it and we have not realized it. And the reason why some have realized it and others have not realized it is not that the nature is different. It is a difference in conditions, and principally a difference between exerting oneself on the path and not exerting oneself on the path. But anyone can become a Buddha.

Question: Rinpoche, I'd like to ask whether it is appropriate to ask in this current situation for some further instruction and guidance on how to work with these techniques in a group situation so that we can better reinforce ourselves in a group rather than just trying to work in isolation?

Rinpoche: Well, what type of group situation do you mean?

Same questioner: A dharma practice group, basically.

Translator: Do you mean people who have received this teaching here?

Same questioner: Yes, primarily yes.

Translator: Primarily, or?

Same questioner: Primarily, other than where Rinpoche authorizes additional people to be there.

Rinpoche: You can do that. You can use this as a regular practice and you can even explain this to other students. Some of them will get it and some of them will not get it, but people can try to practice it.

Question: Rinpoche, there has been a progression of teachings. I'd like to ask about the one where we talk about the nature of occurrence and the nature of stillness as having the same nature—like waves coming from water. But later, when you were talking about spontaneous presence you talked about thoughts arising. I was wondering, in the enlightened state, when thoughts arise, does that mean that thoughts arise, or there is a sort of a looking around at thoughts? In other words, are thoughts coming when we think, or are they spontaneously there and it is just a looking around at these thoughts? Because we've been told they do not come from anywhere and they do not go anywhere, yet they appear. So what makes it possible to survey them like that?

Translator: I may not have understood your question at all, so if this answer does not have anything to do with what you were asking, we will have to try again.

Rinpoche: You talked about the awakened state. In the awakened state there is no thought as we know it, which means no thoughts connected with fixation at all, or joy and displeasure, jealousy, competitiveness, all the kleshas and everything we know of as thought. On the other hand, it is incorrect to simply say there are no thoughts for a Buddha, because, as we understand thought, that is tantamount to saying that a Buddha is an idiot. So what we say is that Buddhas possess among their wisdoms, the wisdom of discrimination, which is the equivalent for Buddhas to what we call thoughts. But it is not conceptual in the heavy-handed way we are familiar with, and it consists of a natural, clear perception of the characteristics of everything around.

Translator: Now was that what you were asking about?

Same questioner: I was wondering whether the progression from water and waves to spontaneous presence was a way of teaching, or was that actually what happens? Is this a progression of having thoughts in our present state? Can we then recognize the nature of their being empty to be spontaneous presence? Is that a different level of enlightenment?

Rinpoche: No, these are just different ways of describing the same nature. They are not describing different levels of experience.

Question: Sir, we have a unique point of view, as for instance, I am standing here so I see things from this specific point of view. And there is a very strong sense of ownership of any particular point of view or a sense of ownership of experience, which also seems to extend to a sense of my experience, my realization. I assume that this is fixated and I am wondering how to work with that specific sense of ownership, that sort of sense of my owning this unique experience?

Rinpoche: The way that you deal with this sense of ownership is the way you deal with the fundamental fixation on a self, from which it springs. There are two ways to tackle this — one is characteristic of the sutras and the other is characteristic of tantra. In the context of the sutras, the only way to deal with this fixation on a self and the resultant sense of perspective or viewpoint; and ownership and all of that, is to analyze this imputation of a self, and through analyzing the self, you determine that it does not exist. Once this determination of its non-existence has become conceptual certainty, then you meditate resting within that certainty produced by analysis, and over a very long period of time this does erase the imputation of a self. The procedure in tantra is different. Rather than analyzing the relationship between the self and that which is owned by or perceived by the self, in Vajrayana we simply determine that all of this fixation comes from our mind. Whatever the fixation manifests as, it starts with our mind. Therefore, we simply look at the mind, and by looking at the mind and determining that the mind has no true existence, you thereby remove the ground from all of this fixation without having to work it out separately in terms of ownership and all of these different issues, and in that way you deal with the whole thing at once.

Question: Rinpoche, I just want to tell you from the bottom of my heart how wonderful it has been to be with you and to hear you and to be filled with these instructions. I feel very blessed. I also feel very strongly about the sangha and the opportunities to be with other practitioners and particularly those who have allowed me, through their dedication and setting up and all the work they do, to bring you here and to allow this to take place,

My question is, Rinpoche, with the realization or knowledge that I possess, hopefully increased by your teachings, I deal with samsara now, and will continue to. We will all go back out into the world, and the softness, the gentility, and this peaceful nature will not necessarily follow us, or if it does, we will not necessarily hear it, see it, smell it, or taste it. My question is related to that. Being doctors, lawyers, philosophers, workers, nurses, practitioners, and being compassionate people wanting to aid and assist others, what ought we to do?

I am particularly thinking of an analogy. Maybe it is because of how I am built, or what I look like, but I seem to have an affinity for bears. When I was in the territories, I encountered a polar bear when I was on a komatick and skiddoo, and fortunately, the komatick did not tip and the skiddoo regained its power and I was able to get away and the bear pretty much stayed in its den. I was very fortunate. About ten years ago, I was up in the northern part of British Columbia and my son and I were out in the woods and a grizzly came on the same path, and we were very fortunate that there was another group of people behind us because we took off, jumped in the water and somehow got away.

Translator: And the bear ate the other people? [laughter]

Same questioner: There were no funerals that I was aware of. The third incident was not too long ago in my home town of Lillooet, in the North. I go out and I have the wonderful opportunity of meditating, walking in the woods and stuff like that, and I still do it; I may be stupid, but I still do it. I was meditating and I was very peaceful and it was just before winter about two years ago. Bears were down feeding from the fruit trees and just going back to get fat like me and relax. A bear came right up by me about fifty meters way, saw me as I saw it from the corner of my eye and I think it just froze. I'd like to think I was just at peace. I do not know, I guess the point of all this is that we go back to samsara, there are different ways of dealing with samsara. We saw in the Vietnam war a Buddhist monk sitting in front or sitting in the center of a boulevard with lots of people and he had doused himself with gasoline and he burned himself alive in protest to the violence happening in his country, to his people, to the spirit of people. We have had indications of people standing in front of tanks, we have had people chaining themselves to trees in the forest. Samsara is working havoc around us. How ought we, given these instructions, to implement them? What do you advise we do, having recognized that all of this is around us? Meditating is one thing. I am wondering if there are other practical ways that we can engage the Buddhadharma? Thank you Rinpoche!

Rinpoche: We need to practice dharma and we need to practice meditation, but we do not place our practice in an environment of blind faith. You still need obviously to retain intelligent sensitivity to what needs to be done in the specific situations that you encounter, both for your own benefit and as it affect others. When you are in a situation where you can practice, where there are no adverse conditions such as rampaging bears [laughter] and other things, then of course, practice as much as you can. But we have to accept— all of us—that as human beings we cannot escape birth, old age, sickness, and death. We are going to experience these things and we are likely to experience a great deal of other unpleasant things along the way. You simply have to maintain in the long term the momentum of your effort to attain liberation, and in the short term, deal appropriately with whatever comes up.

Question: I was wondering if Rinpoche could talk about when it is potentially useful to others to hear of your own specific experiences with mahamudra, and when it may not be useful or may even be potentially harmful, either to self or others?

Rinpoche: There are experiences and experiences; and some types of experiences are pointless to talk about, and other types are helpful to talk about. For example, if through your practice of meditation you start to have hallucinations and see various things, then there is no point in telling other people about that. On the other hand, if through your practice of meditation you gain experience that sometimes your samadhi is clearer and at other times it is not as clear, and when you did such and such a thing it helped it to become clearer and so on, recounting those experiences can be of help to others, because they will hear about what you did that helped you and maybe it will help them too. That will probably not harm them and could possibly help them. Also, talking in a simple and unpretentious way about meditation practice does inspire other people to practice.

11 CONCLUSIONS

THIS TEXT that I have now explained, *Pointing Out the Dharmakaya*, is a very profound text by the Ninth Karmapa, and it bears tremendous blessing. At the same time, as it is the shortest complete presentation of mahamudra practice, it would be very helpful if you were also able to study the longer presentations of mahamudra. This is a way of relying upon the second of the four gurus, the guru who is the dictates of the sugatas, or the teachings of Buddhas and bodhisattvas; because if you study various texts on mahamudra, it will definitely help your view and meditation.

When the Sixteenth Gyalwa Karmapa was in the West he was approached by some of his students and asked, "What are the most beneficial books to translate for the use of future practitioners?" He suggested that the most important text to translate was the text, *Moonbeams of Mahamudra*, by Dagpo Tashi Namgyal (published in English as *Mahamudra: The Quintessence of Mind and Meditation*).[39] He said this out of his understanding of the needs of Westerners, and in particular out of his recognition, and through his great wisdom of what type of practice is appropriate nowadays for people in Western countries.

It was therefore translated and has been published. It is very, very helpful to study this book. I realize that it is somewhat intimidating in its thickness and also in the density of the text itself. Even though on first reading it may be difficult to penetrate, on the second reading you may find things that did not make sense to you the first time which will be very helpful and which you can actually apply to your experience. Maybe things that do not make sense to you the second time will make sense to you the third time you read it. Of course it is very much worthwhile studying the two other mahamudra commentaries [*The Ocean of Definitive Meaning* and *Dispelling the Darkness of Ignorance*] by the Ninth Karmapa, and if you can study these and similar texts it will be very helpful. Of course if you have someone to teach the texts to you, that is best. But even if you do not, you should read them and rely upon them as the guru of the dictates of the sugatas. By studying these texts you will actually learn things that will help your experience of meditation, chiefly by comparing what you have experienced to what is described in the text.

However, the way that you study such texts and the motivation with which you study them are important. You might read these books out of curiosity and the desire to learn something. You might read them with the wish to know all about the person who wrote them and what that person had to say. There is nothing wrong with that in general, because these are dharma books, and so therefore you are learning something about dharma. But this approach to study is principally that of a thinker, someone who speculates. Here we are concerned with the use of study as a way to refine our experience of meditation. Therefore, as you are reading these books you should be looking for things that actually reflect and illuminate your experience. You should be looking for statements or instructions in these texts that will enable you to assess the quality of your experience and enable you to detect possible distractions and diversions and so forth. If you read these texts with the motivation that you are doing so in order to help your practical experience of meditation, then you will discover a great deal in them that will be helpful in just that way. You will come across something that will reveal a point that you have been unable to understand or unable to apply, and you will all of a sudden be certain saying, "Ah, this is how it is!" That is actually receiving the pointing out from the guru who is the dictates of the Sugatas.

Great masters of the past said that dharma texts are "the teacher who never gets mad at you," [laughter] because your relationship with the book is entirely up to you. For example, if you do not understand something and you read it again and again and again, unlike a teacher who might get upset at being asked the same question a hundred times, the book will never get angry at you for reading the same passage again for a hundred times. If while studying the texts you all of a sudden run out of time and have to put the book away abruptly and quickly, the book will never get angry at you for closing it. In that way, this guru who is the dictates of the Sugatas is very convenient to study with and very beneficial to your experience and realization.

Through receiving this instruction and practicing this meditation some of you may have recognized the practice and the nature of your mind. By this I do not mean that I have any particular blessing to bestow, but that these instructions are profound. If you have recognized or you do recognize mind's nature through this practice, do not become arrogant about it; just keep on practicing, keep on meditating. It is possible that some of you are still unsure of how to rest the mind, still unsure how this actually works, and you may not have recognized your mind's nature. In such a case do not become despondent. Do not think, "Oh, I do not understand, I cannot understand, it is hopeless." Simply continue meditating and you will definitely be able to recognize your mind's nature. Even if you have not yet recognized it while receiving these instructions, you certainly can recognize it through doing the practice. And some of you may have not gained what you consider a decisive recognition. Even if you haven't gained a recognition yet, if you keep on practicing, gradually your experience will become clearer and clearer, and the recognition will become decisive. It is worthwhile pursuing this, because up to now we have never entered the path that will lead to Buddhahood. We have simply wandered around in samsara restlessly and pointlessly, and now you are entering the path that leads to full Buddhahood, which once begun will never be lost. Depending upon your diligence, the habit of this path will increase quickly or slowly, and you will attain Buddhahood quickly or slowly, but you will definitely attain it and therefore you are very fortunate. The opportunity to practice is precious because the prerequisite for recognition is taming your own mind, and the most effective way to do this is through mahamudra practice.

In general, I've talked a lot about the view and meditation, and not very much about conduct. But that doesn't mean that the implementation of appropriate conduct is unimportant. We need, of course, to practice meditation and cultivate the view, but when we're not actually practicing, we need to pay attention to our mode of conduct because even though we practice meditation, we could still engage in rough modes of conduct, we could still be harbouring malicious intentions. It's necessary, even while you're practicing this type of meditation, to continue to increase your compassion for others; you should engage in whatever methods you can of accumulating merit, such as making offerings and being generous; to increase your confidence in and sacred outlook towards the dharma itself and the instructions you have received; to continue to cultivate the practices of guru yoga and the meditation upon various deities. All of these things have great benefit, and all of these things coming together with meditation will make the practice both profound and effective. When you're engaged in your post-meditation activities, whatever they may be, bring to bear as much mindfulness and alertness as you can, and try and bring the wisdom of meditation into them. And as much as you can, let go of anger and jealousy and arrogance; as much as you can, try to increase your loving kindness and compassion for others, your motivation of bodhichitta. If you do these things, not only will your practice flourish, but you will succeed in your mundane endeavours as well; and in your mundane endeavours, you will never contradict the dharma, you will never be at cross-purposes with your practice or your path. Therefore, in post-meditation, try to bring the samadhi, the meditative absorption, of your meditation practice into your activities, and, especially, maintain a good and kind motivation, being careful not to come under the sway of negative or malicious motivation.

You're extremely fortunate to have entered the gate of dharma, and in particular to have the opportunity to perform this practice. If you look back on your life up to now, you may find some episodes in your life that you would rather forget, things you did that you wish you had not done. But you don't need to torment yourself about these negative actions, because, in your present situation, you have the necessary resources to transcend them. Rather than tormenting yourself about what you did in the past, you could rejoice in the opportunity you have now to transcend negative patterns. We are ordinary people, and as ordinary people, it's natural that, from time to time, we look back with feelings of guilt. We may fear that we might do those things again. That's all right, but there is a better way to deal with such feelings. If you practice, the power and the momentum of your practice, together with a strong commitment on your part to change, will give you the ability to do so. Whatever you've done that you don't want to do again, whatever you've said, and whatever you've thought, no matter how negative or miserable you have been in your life, you can transcend it. By practicing and maintaining a firm commitment, you will gradually purify all of these patterns and habits.

From time to time, reading certain books may help, in particular *The Jewel Ornament of Liberation*, and especially the chapter in that book on the perfection of wisdom. Gampopa was an extraordinary teacher, the great disciple and lineage holder of Milarepa. He had extraordinary experience and realization of meditation and the teachings, and, in a sense, his whole experience and realization are summed up in *The Jewel Ornament of Liberation*. The chapter on the perfection of wisdom is not so much guidance for meditating on the mind's nature, as instruction for the understanding and contemplation of emptiness. But it's very effective, very beneficial. If you study that chapter, and even recite the words, that will bring some benefit.

Dedication

I know that all of you have come here at the expense of the various things you would otherwise have been doing. I know that you all have a lot of work to do. You all have homes and families that you have to take care of. And you cast all these things aside and came here to this somewhat isolated place to listen to me tell you what I know about these teachings. In doing so, you've given me the opportunity to at least pass on what I've heard from my teachers. This has been delightful for me, and I am confident that it has benefited everyone involved. I would like to thank you for this opportunity.

Based on my experience, there's no deception in the actual practice of these instructions. I can speak from experience that these practices are helpful. If I were to say to you, "I'm going to protect you from the lower realms through the power of my compassion and my miraculous abilities," I would be lying to you. But if, on the other hand, I say to you, "I can guarantee that these practices are genuine, trustworthy, and really helpful," that's not a lie. So please practice.

It has been said by all of the great teachers of the past that any practice one does needs to embody what is called the threefold excellence. The first aspect of this is the excellence in the beginning, or the excellence as a preliminary, which is the generation of bodhichitta as your intention or motivation for doing the practice. The second excellence is called the excellence in between, which is maintaining a degree of non-conceptuality and being without much fixation on the contents of meditation during the entire practice. Finally, the conclusion is called the excellent conclusion, which is the dedication of all the merit or virtue of the practice to all sentient beings, which is a further extension of being without attachment to the practice itself. Therefore, in order that we conform to this format of threefold excellence, we will now dedicate the merit. While doing so please think that you give away all of the virtue you have accumulated through this teaching to all beings without exception.

OUTLINE OF THE ROOT TEXT
Pointing Out the Dharmakaya

I. The Preliminaries

THE GENERAL PRELIMINARIES

1. Difficulty of finding a free and well-favored situation
2. The contemplation of impermanence
3. The contemplation of karma and its results
4. The contemplation of the retribution of samsara

THE SPECIAL PRELIMINARIES

1. The instruction on taking refuge and arousing bodhichitta
2. The meditation and recitation practice of Vajrasattva
3. The instruction on the mandala practice
   a. The shrine mandala
   b. The offering mandala
4. The guru yoga that quickly brings blessings

THE SUPERIOR PRELIMINARIES [the four conditions]

1. The causal condition: Revulsion of samsara
2. The principal condition: Reliance upon the guru
   a. A guru of the lineage
   b. The dictates of the Sugatas
   c. The guru of dharmata [or absolute truth]
   d. The sign guru of appearances
3. The focal condition: Direct recognition of the mind's nature
4. The immediate condition: The absence of hope or anxiety about one's progress in meditation

II. The Main Part
Shamatha Meditation

1. Points of body
1. Points of mind
   a. General points of mind
   b. Particular points of mind
      i. Holding the mind on a visual object
      ii Holding the mind on other sensory objects
      iii. Eliminating sunkenness and wildness
      iv. Holding the mind on no support
      v. Holding the mind based on the breath
      vii. Holding the mind based on counting
      - Tightening, loosening, and turning away
      - Increasing shamatha and the recognition of it

Vipashyana Meditation

1. Looking
   a. Looking at stillness
   b. Looking at occurrence
   c. Looking at appearances
   d. Looking at body and mind as the same or different
   e. Looking at stillness and occurrence as the same or different
2. Pointing out
   a. Pointing out stillness
   b. Pointing out occurrence
   c. Pointing out appearances
   d. Pointing out body and mind as the same or different
   e. Pointing out stillness and occurrence as the same or different

III. The Conclusion

1. Enhancing the practice and dispelling hindrances
2. The way that virtues arise and the way of proceeding along the path
3. The way of realizing the fruition

NOTES

1. The Kagyu lineage supplication is called the *Dorje Chang Tungma* in Tibetan. Thrangu Rinpoche has written an extensive commentary on this prayer in *Showing the Path to Liberation.* The Kagyu lineage prayer with the visualization can be obtained from Namo Buddha Publications.

2. Penkar Jampal Zangpo was a disciple of the Sixth Karmapa who accomplished realization by practicing the instructions received from the Karmapa. After he accomplished realization, he composed this prayer and went on to become the teacher of the Seventh Karmapa.

3. The ultimate or supreme siddhi is the stable realization of the radiant clarity or clear light nature of mind and all reality which we know as complete and perfect enlightenment or Buddhahood. The relative siddhis are such qualities as loving kindness, compassion, intelligence, the wisdom of insight, spiritual power, protection, the removal of obstacles, good health, longevity, wealth and magnetism etc. — *Thrangu Rinpoche (TR)*

4. This section was taken from Thrangu Rinpoche's talk in Ojai in 1993.

5. All meditation can be divided into the two categories of tranquility meditation (shamatha) and insight meditation (vipashyana). Vipashyana, in turn, can be divided into the vipashyana of the sutra tradition and the vipashyana of the mahamudra tradition. In the sutra tradition, there is analytical vipashyana and placement meditation. In the mahamudra, or tantric, tradition, vipashyana is based on the direct pointing out of the nature of mind and the nature of things by a fully qualified and experienced holder of the mahamudra lineage. — LTN

6. It is important to understand that the term *prajna* includes in one term the notions of knowledge, wisdom, and primordial awareness or transcendental awareness, which is the highest form of prajna. Worldly knowledge — medicine, literature, business management, economics or anthropology — is one form of prajna. Knowledge of the teachings of the Buddha and other enlightened beings is spiritual prajna. Both worldly and spiritual prajna are based on the acquisition of information, and though they may have a great deal of practical benefit, they will not by themselves liberate one from the root causes of suffering. Only the highest form of prajna, jnana — primordial awareness, which is liberated from the superimposition on experience of perceiver and perceived — will free one from the root causes of suffering. — *Lama Tashi Namgyal (LTN)*

7. The Vajrayana teachings are often called this and Rinpoche has said that they are basically the same. He has said that the word often translated as "secret" should be translated as "essential," so it would be the essential mantra Vajrayana.

8. A free and well favoured situation is to be born with eight freedoms and ten opportunities (*tal jor*). *Tal* is often translated as "freedom" and *jor* as "endowments," "qualities," "resources," or "opportunities" which constitute a precious human birth to practice dharma. The eight freedoms are traditionally enumerated as freedom from birth as a hell being, a hungry ghost, an animal, a barbarian, a long-lived god, a heretic, a mentally handicapped person, or living in a dark age (here meaning when no Buddha has come, in other contexts, according to the teachings on five degenerations we are living in a dark age). Of the ten conjunctions or resources, the five personal conjunctions are having a human body, being born in a land to which the dharma has spread, having all of one's senses intact, not reverting to evil ways, and having confidence in the three jewels. (Having one's senses impaired to the extent that one's mind could not function properly in the study and practice of dharma would constitute the loss of one's precious human birth.) The five conjunctions that come by way of others are that a Buddha has been born in this age, that the Buddha taught the dharma, that the dharma still exists, that there are still followers who have realized the meaning and essence of the teachings of the dharma, and there are benevolent sponsors. — *LTN*

9. There are three main traditions in Buddhism, Hinayana, Mahayana, and Vajrayana. While Tibetan Buddhists actually practice all three levels, Tibet is one of the few traditionally Buddhist countries which practices the Vajrayana.

10. Blessing is the process by which one individual introduces some of their accumulated merit into another's "stream of being." The ability to bestow blessing depends on the donor's degree of spiritual attainment and on the recipient's faith. The donor is usually the root guru, whose blessing is said to contain that of all the sources of refuge combined. Although future experiences are largely shaped by present actions, the root guru's blessing can partially modify this. That is, it can create conditions favourable to the maturation of any religious pre-dispositions our past actions may have generated, giving us the inspiration and energy we require to begin practising. In this way, unless our acts have been extremely unwholesome, the guru's blessing can help us overcome conflicting emotions and other obstacles. Thus the guru's blessing helps us realize the Buddha-potential we all possess.

11. This is from the *Chariot of Deliverance: The Supreme Path* by the Ninth Karmapa.

12. The English term for this might be "transcendental compassion," meaning compassion not just for a few persons, but for all sentient beings. In the Sanskrit *bodhi* means "awakened" or "enlightened" and *chitta* means "mind," so bodhichitta means awakened mind. Many translators prefer "awakened" over "enlightened" because the word enlightened is a non-Buddhist term that was first used when Buddhism was introduced. In Tibetan this "awakened mind" was translated as *chang chup kyi sem* in which *chang chup* means "awakened" and *kyi* is a conjunction and *sem* is mind. So the Tibetan translators translated the Sanskrit quite literally into Tibetan

The generation of bodhichitta is based on the altruistic wish to bring about the welfare, and ultimately the total liberation, of all sentient beings from all forms of suffering. What distinguishes bodhichitta from the ordinary compassionate aspirations to benefit others shared by all people of good will is the recognition that one cannot ultimately fulfill these aspirations until one has attained the state of mental purification and liberation of Buddhahood, which is the source of all positive qualities, including the omniscience that can see, individual by individual, the causes of suffering and the causes and path of liberation from suffering. This understanding gives rise at some point to the initial generation of the aspiration to attain the state of Buddhahood in order to liberate all sentient beings from suffering and to establish them all in states of happiness. This is called aspiration bodhichitta, which must be followed by what is called the bodhichitta of entering or perseverance bodhichitta, which is the training in loving-kindness, compassion, the six paramitas or transcendent perfections, etc., which lead to the attainment of Buddhahood. Aspiration bodhichitta and perseverance bodhichitta are both included in the term relative bodhichitta. Absolute bodhichitta is direct insight into the ultimate nature. This state of primordial awareness *is* compassion and loving-kindness and gives rise spontaneously and without preconception to compassionate activity. — *LTN*

13. The ten non-virtuous actions are taking life, taking what is not given, sexual misconduct, lying, sowing discord, harsh words, worthless chatter, covetousness, wishing harm to others, and wrong views. Acts are regarded as non-virtuous or unwholesome when they result in undesirable karmic effects. Thus, this list of ten unwholesome acts occurs generally in discussions of the functioning of karma. The first three are actions of body, the next four of speech, and the last three of mind. The ten virtuous actions are the opposites of the above ten non-virtuous actions.

14. The five actions of immediate consequence are: killing one's father, killing one's mother, killing an arhat, intentionally wounding a Buddha and causing them to bleed, and creating a schism in the sangha. They are called actions which have an immediate result at death in that they are the cause ripening at death which results in rebirth in a hell realm.

15. Upon enlightenment, all one's karma is dissolved as there is no basis for it. However on a more general level, purification refers mainly to the changing of conditions which then lighten the result of one's karma. Karma means causes, conditions and results. We cannot change the cause of an action or avoid its result, e.g., when one plants sesame seeds, the results are always sesame plants. However, through purification, a result which may have been the loss of our life may only be a small injury.

16. In this practice one visualizes a flow of amrita, or elixir, of awareness flowing from the seed syllable HUNG, surrounded by the hundred-syllable mantra on a moon disc in Vajrasattva's heart. All one's harmful deeds and obscurations are purified by this flow of amrita into one's body.

17. The four powers, according to Jamgon Kongtrul Lodro Thaye, in *The Torch of Certainty*, are: (1) "the power to renounce" and regret your previous misdeeds [mentally before the Three Jewels and the Three Roots] as vigorously as if you had swallowed poison; (2) "the power to refuse to repeat a harmful deed," and to firmly resolve, "even if my life is at stake, I will never do it again"; (3) "the power to rely" on taking

refuge and engendering the enlightened attitude; and (4) "the power to carry out all types of remedial wholesome acts to purify harmful ones," including the "six gates of remedy," and others, and so on. The six gates of remedy are to say the names of Buddhas and bodhisattvas; to set up images, hold books, and stupas; to make offerings to the Buddha, dharma, and sangha, and to the lama, yidam, and dakas, dakinis, and dharma protectors; to recite the sutras and tantras taught by the Buddha; to recite the "hundred-syllable mantra of the Tathagata," the mantras of Vairochana, Akshobhya, and other profound mantras; confident in the potentiality of Buddhahood, while meditating and reciting, to meditate on the significance of non-self (emptiness) and threefold purity, i.e., without regard for the obscurations to be purified, an instrument of purification, and a purifier, and between meditation sessions, to concentrate on the unreality, or illusoriness of all phenomena.

18. *Bag chaks*; the karmic seeds or imprints stored in our minds from our actions of body, speech and mind which are carried from one life to the next. They ripen dependent on appropriate conditions which are then projected as our experiences of both internal and external phenomena. Also as habitual patterns they are the determining factor in how we respond to our experiences.

19. When you talk about guru in the Mahamudra lineage, there is the pure (dharmakaya) aspect of the guru, the distance lineage gurus, and the close lineage gurus. The distance lineage gurus start with the Lord Buddha and extend in a continuous, unbroken succession of enlightened masters and students all the way down to the Karmapa. We call that the distance lineage because it goes all the way back to the Buddha Shakyamuni.

There is the close lineage of Mahamudra as well. That lineage begins with the Buddha Vajradhara, who bestowed Mahamudra teachings on the bodhisattva Lodro Rinchen, which teachings then come down to Tilopa and Naropa. In the case of the great masters who received Mahamudra lineage transmissions directly from the Buddha Vajradhara, those transmissions happened a long time after Prince Siddhartha's parinirvana. The physical Buddha, the historical Buddha Shakyamuni, Prince Siddhartha, was at the time no longer in physical Prince Siddhartha form. What happened was that first these great masters received the teachings of the Buddha and the Buddha's disciples through "distance lineages," and they practiced them. Through their practice they attained realization. As part of their realization the Buddha manifested to them, but not as Prince Siddhartha, as Buddha Vajradhara. So, Buddha, the sambhogakaya of the Buddha, and the nirmanakaya of the Buddha, which is Prince Siddhartha in our case. The Buddha Vajradhara means all in one — the ever-present Buddha, the timeless Buddha.

Then the Buddha Vajradhara transmitted directly to certain great masters, but only as a result of the realization of the teachings they had already received from their masters, whose teachings started with the historical Buddha. In this way, the Mahamudra lineage and many Vajrayana Buddhist lineages actually have distance lineage as well as close lineage. — *Tai Situ Rinpoche (TSR)*

20. Traditionally the notion of revulsion is the aversion to samsaric existence that arises with the growing perception of the inevitable sufferings of conditioned existence. When one's understanding of impermanence leads one to conclude that even the transitory happiness and pleasures of conditioned existence inevitably deteriorate and

disappear—and that because of our clinging to them, this process is of the nature of suffering—then one's mind develops deep aversion to and revulsion for conditioned existence and begins to seek liberation from it.—*LTN*

21. "The common vehicle" is a way of referring to those teachings held in common by all traditions of Buddhism, which are the teachings on personal liberation of the Hinayana, or lesser vehicle.

22. The fivefold posture is: first the that the body should be "as straight as an arrow," which means the back should be straight and not leaning; second, the chin should be bent slightly inward like a hook; the third point is that the legs should be crossed (full lotus is best or else half lotus); fourth is that the body "should be gathered together like chains," which means lock it in position as with iron shackles, the way to do this is to join the hands, placing them the width of four fingers below the navel; fifth is to keep one's mind and body reasonably tight, exerting a certain amount of effort so the body and mind are composed and focused.

    This is the preferred posture of Marpa, who said if one can keep the body in this posture, the subtle energy circulating in the body would be ideal and would then actually circulate through the central channel of the body.

23. In Tibetan medicine and meditation the body contains numerous subtle channels (Skt. *nadi*, Tib. *tsa*) which are not anatomical in nature, but more like channels in acupuncture. There are thousands of channels but the three main channels are the central channel, which runs roughly along the spinal column, and the left and right channels either side of this. Prana is the energy, or "wind," moving through the nadis. As is said, "Mind consciousness rides the horse of prana on the pathways of the nadis. The bindu is mind's nourishment."

    Because of dualistic thinking, prana enters the left and right channels. This divergence of energy in the subtle body corresponds to the mental activity that falsely distinguishes between subject and object and leads to karmically determined activity. Through yogic practice, the pranas can be brought into the central channel and therefore transformed into wisdom-prana. Then the mind can recognize its fundamental nature, realizing all dharmas as unborn [empty].

24. There are two subtle channels inside the throat, and if they are bent slightly forward, the energy will circulate in them reducing mental agitation in one's meditation.

25. As with the syllables, these three spheres of light are meant to be visualized simultaneously directly in front of one, one below the other, with the white sphere on top. —*LTN*

26. A Vajrayana term for a kind of psychic heat generated and experienced through certain meditative practices. This heat serves to burn up all the types of obstacles and confusion. One of the Six Dharmas of Naropa.

27. This technique should not be practiced without the guidance of a qualified instructor who has practiced this technique successfully him or herself.—*LTN*

28. Sometimes these stages are enumerated as four: waterfall, fast moving river in a narrow ravine, slowly flowing river, still ocean without waves.—*LTN*

29. It is quite useful, for instance, to tighten your muscles by using force to straighten your posture. — *LTN*

30. Lucidity, clarity, cognitive clarity, cognitive capacity, and luminosity are used as interchangeable translations of *salwa* in this text. — *LTN*

31. One who, according to the Hinayana teachings, has attained individual salvation or individual liberation from suffering. — *LTN*

32. One supplicates principally the lama as the source of all blessing, the transmitter of the enlightened awareness and energy of the lineage, the embodiment of all the Buddhas and bodhisattvas of the three times and ten directions, and the embodiment of the three roots — lama, yidam, and dakas, dakinis, and dharma protectors. — *LTN*

33. The "truth" or correctness of the thought from the standpoint of conventional understanding is not the point here. Whether Mary is really a Democrat is not the point; in this technical sense of the term relative truth, the thought, whether correct or incorrect, is still a relative truth. In either case, it is a conceptual imputation. — *LTN*

34. There is, of course, a great incentive for beginners to look at thoughts of anger, because anger is so vexatious and causes so much trouble in one's life. It is much more difficult to remember to look at the mind when it is experiencing feelings of attachment, happiness, love, pleasure, etc., because these emotions are not generally experienced as vexatious. Nevertheless, the attachment associated with these experiences sooner or later, when they change or are disrupted, becomes the basis of suffering. Therefore, it is very important to develop one's mindfulness and train one's mind to look directly and nakedly at thoughts that we experience as happiness as well. — *LTN*

35. Storehouse consciousness was an early attempt to translate *alaya vijnana* — translated variously as all-basis consciousness, alaya consciousness, ground consciousness and the eighth consciousness — the conceptual notion of a consciousness where all the karmic latencies created by our dualistic actions are stored as potential primary causes of experience until such time as secondary conditions spark their ripening in our experience. The alaya vijnana, while it is a useful notion to have when seeking to understand the cause and effect of karmic actions, is also in its nature empty. — *LTN*

36. The teachings of the sutras form the basis of the student's question. — *LTN*

37. What is here being translated as "conduct," in many of Chogyam Trungpa Rinpoche's teachings and translations is translated as "action." — *LTN*

38. Bearing in mind what Rinpoche has been teaching in the paragraph immediately prior to this quotation and bearing in mind Rinpoche's answer to the first question following this section on this subject, it is important to recognize that this is not a definitive statement. — *LTN*

39. This book was published by Shambhala Publications.